YOUNG FACES OF HOLINESS

MODERN SAINTS IN PHOTOS AND WORDS

YOUNG FACES OF HOLINESS

MODERN SAINTS IN PHOTOS AND WORDS

ANN BALL

Our Sunday Visitor Publishing Division
Our Sunday Visitor, Inc.
Huntington, Indiana 46750

Our Sunday Visitor Publishing Division
Our Sunday Visitor, Inc.
200 Noll Plaza, Huntington, IN 46750

ISBN: 1-931709-55-6 (Inventory No. T32)
LCCN: 2003113170

Cover design by Tyler Ottinger
Interior design by Robert L. Hoffman

PRINTED IN THE UNITED STATES OF AMERICA

DEDICATION

This book is lovingly dedicated to all the children of America and to the parents, relatives, priests, and religious charged with guiding them towards sanctity.

"Whoever receives one such child in my name receives me" (Matthew 18:5).

DECLARATION OF OBEDIENCE

Not all the people in this book have been declared saints. The header of each chapter indicates if the person is a saint, a blessed, or a venerable. When no title is shown, the person is properly called a servant of God.

In loving obedience to the decrees of several Roman Pontiffs, in particular those of Pope Urban VIII, I declare that I in no way intend to prejudge Holy Mother Church in the matter of saints, sanctity, miracles, etc. Final authority in such matters rests with the See of Rome, to whose judgment I willingly submit.

The Author

TABLE OF CONTENTS

INTRODUCTION

When my friend Father Campion Lally, O.F.M., wrote me from Japan to suggest I write a book on the youth candidates for canonization and children with a reputation for holiness, I thought, "No way!" In order to be a candidate, they have to be dead. The thought of an entire book about dead children disturbed me. In addition, I thought their lives would be too much the same. After all, how much living can someone do before the age of twenty?

Then I reread some lines from A. E. Housman's poem, "To an Athlete Dying Young." In his ode to the young athlete, the poet says "Smart lad, to slip betimes away, from fields where glory does not stay." How true. Earthly glory is nothing; the glory of eternity is what we all should strive for.

Although many of the youth in this book suffered terribly with great physical pain before their deaths, they all have in common a heroic cheerfulness and spirit of giving. In the wisdom of their inno-cent youth, they provide clarity for our own path at the end of our days. In just a brief time, they have internalized the true joy of the cross — the value of suffering — and have lived in a constant effort to accept and follow God's will and His plan for them. Some are martyrs. The child who spills his or her blood for Christ does not leave us in any doubt as to his or her sanctity.

Can a child who is not a martyr, technically called a confessor, be a saint? Since the beginning of the Roman

"Jesus Christ Morning Star"
AN ICON OF CHRIST AS A TEENAGER
BY REV. WILLIAM HART MCNICHOLS

canonization process in the eleventh century, few children who were not martyrs were accorded the honors of the altar. The first among those younger than twenty-one years of age was Saint Stanislaus Kostka, who died in 1568 at the age of eighteen and was canonized in 1726. Later, in 1963, the young Italian laborer Nunzio Sulpricio, who died in 1837 at the age of nineteen, was beatified by Pope Paul VI. The youngest non-martyr saint is Saint Dominic Savio, who died in 1857 at the age of fourteen and was canonized in 1954.

In May 2000, the beatification of the two child seers from Fátima marked the first non-martyr children so young (Francisco died at age ten and Jacinta at age nine) ever to be accorded this honor. Although child canonizations were rare, the beatification of the Marto children confirmed a belief that the church has had since the time of Christ — that children have received the love of God in a way befitting youngsters. As the Second Vatican Council pointed out, "Children also have their own apostolic work to do. In their own way, they can be true living witnesses to Christ among their companions" (Decree on the Apostolate of the Laity). As Pope Saint Pius X had predicted years before, "There will be saints among the children." Commenting on this prophecy of his predecessor, our own Pope John Paul II said, "Now there will be apostles among the children."

We must recognize that to fulfill this, a child must have the holiness of a child, not that of an adult. True sanctity, heroic sanctity, generally associated in such a short life span with those who have suffered heroically during an illness, must appear in the measure and in the modality that corresponds to childhood.

Thus, there is a marvelous holiness proper to children in their own manner, and not in the manner of adults. This results in some extraordinary friends of God of a tender age. God certainly wants to have special friends who are children. And to children, he presents models of their own age to inspire them in ways other than martyrdom.

In this book, we present brief sketches of the lives of many holy children and youth, all under the age of twenty. It is our hope that those who read this book will find one whose charisma attracts them and go on to learn more about that person, thereby acquiring a new young friend in heaven.

1

Alexia González-Barros
Spain, 1971–1985

To Do What Jesus Wants

The patient in the crisp white hospital bed was obviously very ill. A large metal device was fitted to her head and neck with screws, and she had been given a medication that turned her mouth purple. She turned to her visitor and said, "First, they made me look like Frankenstein, now I look more like Dracula!" In spite of the horror of Alexia's condition, the friend had no option but to laugh at the young teen's comment. To visitors, Alexia always presented a cheerful demeanor, turning the conversation to them and away from her own problems. One of her doctors brought his students to see her, telling them, "I want you to see how it is to be joyful, despite pain and suffering."

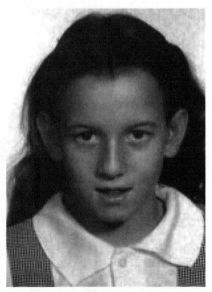

Alexia González-Barros

Alexia González-Barros died of cancer in 1985 at the age of fourteen. This Spanish teenager accepted her fatal illness, kept a cheerful sense of humor, offered her suffering for others, and faithfully lived her motto and constant prayer: "Jesus, may I always do what you want."

Alexia had once begun a school paper with the words, "To serve is to live joyfully." In her suffering, she attempted to serve God always with joy. Alexia's cause for beatification has been entered at Rome.

Her story is detailed in *Faces of Holiness II*. ✦

2

Venerable Anne de Guigné
France, 1911–1922

Model of Obedience

When she was a young child, no one could have suspected that Anne de Guigné would one day be a candidate for the honors of the altar. Frankly, this oldest of the four children of the Count Jacques de Guigné was a little tyrant and a bit of a hellion to boot. Although loving, intelligent and frank, she could be tempestuous and display an iron will in order to get her own way.

While still in the crib, Anne once imperiously told a doctor called to examine her to "take your hat and go!" Out of jealousy, she rubbed sand in her new baby brother's eyes. She was a natural leader, but with the other children she sometimes pushed rather than led. For the first years of her life, Anne's will was directed only to the things Anne wanted. When she was four, however, things changed and Anne began to direct her will to the things God wanted, instead of her own wishes. In a child's way, she began to walk the way of perfection.

———

Anne was born April 25, 1911, at the Chateau de la Cour, the family home of Count de Guigné and his wife, Countess Antoinette de Charette. The chateau overlooks the Lake of Annecy in one of the most beautiful parts of Savoy. The baby girl was baptized Jeanne Marie Josephine Anne, but her family called her Nenette. Her birth was followed by those of her siblings, Jacques, Madeleine, and Marie Antoinette. Just as Anne was called by a nickname, the long names of the others were shortened to JoJo, Leleine, and Marinette. It was among her brother and sisters and the family servants that Anne began her little apostolate of love and obedience which one day may lead her to the honors of the altar.

Anne came from a long line of noble kings and soldiers. Her father was an exemplary Christian and a patriot. A soldier himself, he had retired at the time of his marriage to dedicate himself to family life.

However, at the outbreak of war in 1915 he rejoined his old regiment, the Chasseurs Alpins, and left for the front.

Three times he was injured and sent home; each time he returned to the defense of his country. The first two times his wounds were not too serious, and Anne was happy to play nurse for her beloved father. The third time an operation at the hospital in Lyons was called for. Madame de Guigné went to see him, taking Anne along. The young girl seemed awed by the sense of suffering of the men in the long lines of white beds. Her mother explained that the men were suffering for France, and the child began to realize some hard truths of life.

On July 30, 1915, Anne awoke to see her mother standing by her bed with red eyes from a night of tears. Then came the awful news: "Daddy is dead." From the day of her father's death, Anne changed. It seemed as if his sacrifice rained down a shower of grace, and the young child cooperated with God's gift in faithful measure. She began by comforting her mother and encouraging her siblings to do so as well. She had realized that to reach God we must be good, and all her thoughts began to turn to making others happy and helping them to be good.

That fall, when the family went to their house in Cannes for the winter, her mother allowed Anne to join the catechism class at the Auxiliatrice Convent. Her teacher, Mother Saint Raymond, was surprised at the depth of the spirituality of this tiny child. Anne's understanding of the lessons, her self-control, and her careful examination of conscience showed that she was ready, at this early age, to receive the Sacrament. Her confessor agreed with Anne's mother and the nuns that she was prepared. The Bishop, however, objected when he saw the name of a child of five on the list of first communicants. The sisters argued in her defense, but the Bishop agreed only on condition that Anne pass an examination by the Superior of the Jesuits, Father Louis Perroy.

Anne was small for her age and on seeing her, the learned Jesuit remarked, "Really it is rather absurd to present such a baby. The mothers will soon want them to make their First Communion before they can walk!" He rapidly changed his mind, however, when he began to examine the little petitioner. Not only did she know her catechism perfectly, but she had a deep understanding of it. Her answers were not merely rote repetition. Father Perroy gave his verdict to Mother

Saint Raymond: "I wish you and I were as well prepared to receive our Lord as this little girl is."

Joyously, Anne joined the others at the first communicants' retreat at the convent. The director of the retreat pointed out that "obedience is the sanctity of children." For Anne, this text became a guideline for the rest of her short life. For her, obedience even in the smallest of things was a direct road to the God she loved.

Anne made her First Communion on March 26, 1917. In her childish hand we can read her First Communion resolution, which she placed on the altar of the church: "I will always obey." Although Anne never talked of this first meeting with Our Lord, it apparently filled her heart with a deep love and gratitude. One day, her governess found her kneeling in a corner, praying. When questioned as to what she was doing, Anne replied, "I was only thanking Jesus for being so kind as to come into my heart."

Suspecting that Anne's relations with Our Lord were more than ordinary, Mother Saint Raymond once asked her, casually, if Our

The smile that attracted all who knew her

Lord ever said anything to her. Anne hesitated for a moment, as if unwilling to tell a secret, then answered, "Not always, but sometimes when I am very quiet." Questioned as to what He said, she hesitated again and responded, "He tells me that He loves me." Another time, Anne's aunt, the superior of the convent, questioned her on the same subject. Anne confided, "Jesus says he loves me. He says He loves me much more than I love Him."

Slowly, Anne began to build a true spirit of sacrifice. Suffering from some childhood illnesses, she put up with a number of unpleasant cures such as mustard poultices and bland food. Her habitual prayer became, "Jesus, I offer it to You." Later, she began to deny herself in the little ways available to a child her age such as giving up some of the delicious sweets offered for dessert, playing the games the other children wanted to play instead of those she preferred, staying home

Anne at nine months

from an outing to keep company with her sick sister or brother, or giving up her toys to the others. "I don't care what they do to me as long as they are good," she said. Even at her tender age, she was concerned that her siblings become good, for she knew that goodness led to God.

The love of God in Anne's young heart spilled out in charity to others. She was especially solicitous of her governess, Madeleine Basset, and the servants of the household. Often, the fruits of her self-denial, the lovely desserts she passed up, were passed along to the maids. Once there was a fire in the village and one poor woman with four children was left homeless. Upset when she heard of it, Anne began to try and think of something that a small girl could do to help. At last, she conceived of a plan. She and "the others" (her way of referring to her brother and sisters) would hold a bazaar and give the profit to the poor, homeless mother. She encouraged the others to deny themselves and save their sweets. Then, with her clever little fingers, she began to make a number of hand-crafted items which she thought people might buy at a bazaar. When at last the little crew thought they had enough, Anne asked her mother's permission to have a bazaar and invite everyone to come with full purses.

The children erected little stalls on the lawn. The refreshment buffet was well stocked with sweets, candied fruits and little cakes the children had saved from their own dessert. There were also dishes of blackberries, nuts, and other good things that the children had gathered from the woods and the garden. A flower stall displayed daisies, dandelions, and various wild flowers for sale at exorbitant prices. Best of all was the handicraft stall, which displayed tiny cradles scooped out of acorns, little baskets carved from horse chestnuts, bags woven of rushes, and other items Anne had made herself. The enthusiastic visitors cleared the stalls, and the eight-year-old organizer was rewarded with the remarkable sum of thirty francs. The homeless woman was very touched to learn that Anne had not simply asked her mother for the money but had worked hard to earn it.

Another time, the children learned that the rabbits at the convent at Annecy had died. This touched Anne's tender heart, and she convinced "the others" to ask permission to open their money boxes and use the funds for the purchase of more rabbits. Of course they were given permission, and the following day the little group purchased a pair of rabbits and happily presented them to the convent.

Brought up in the midst of wealth, Anne had a great respect for workers and a great sympathy for the poor. Following a suggestion of her mother's, she learned to knit in order to make some scarves and other small things to be donated to the poor. She tried hard to make these as good as possible, saying, "It must be well-done if it is for the poor children." When her mother made up the packages to be taken to them, Anne used to add some of her nicest dolls and toys, not the old broken ones.

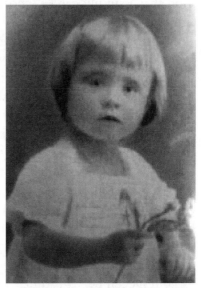

At two and a half she loved flowers

Although she led a sheltered life, Anne was aware that sin existed, and she asked the nuns to give her a soul to convert, preferably a "really big sinner." With all her strong will and determination, Anne would pray for "her sinner" until success was reported.

Although she was intelligent, there were some school subjects which were difficult for Anne and which she disliked intensely. She worked hard at them anyway, telling a little friend, "Our work is a present that we can give Jesus. So when it seems hard, just think that now you have something for Him. Nothing costs much when we love Him."

In her resolutions after a retreat when she was nine, we read: "How shall I do it? How shall I overcome the obstacles? ... These are my faults: I am inclined to be proud and to be lazy, so a daily struggle is necessary for me." At ten, Anne wrote, "I will imitate the little

Jesus. If the time (in class) seems long, I will offer God the effort. . . . It depends on me. Mother cannot do the work for me."

Although Anne had a precocious spirituality at an early age and was a very holy little girl, she was, after all, a child. At one point, both she and one of her sisters had decided that they wanted to become nuns when they grew up. "We must practice the sort of things we shall have to do when we enter the convent," the older sister told the young aspirant. Shortly thereafter the girls were found in the dairy solemnly taking deep breaths over a new cheese. Questioned, Anne explained that they were smelling the cheese "because it isn't very nice." This was their childish thought of mortification, and led to quite a bit of amusement on the part of the adults.

In the last year of her life, Anne discussed many things with her friend Simone. This girl later testified, "Nenette had such love of God that I simply can't describe it." Anne seemed to know that her time was short, although she was not ill.

During the summer and fall of 1921, a strangely sweet peace seemed to be filling Anne's soul, and this was noticed by some of those around her. When the girls parted that fall, as they did each year, her friend said, "I shall never see her again. I am sure God is going to take her; she doesn't seem to belong to this world any more."

When Anne was eight, she began to have severe headaches caused by a spinal weakness. Although the trouble was supposed to have been cured, the headaches returned in December of 1921. At first, the doctors did not consider the problem to be serious. As the others played, Anne would sit in the garden by her governess, seemingly happy in spite of the pain. She once told Mademoiselle, "We have lots of joys here on earth, but they do not last; the only joy that lasts is to have made a sacrifice."

On December 19, Anne came down to supper, but her headache became so severe that she had to return to her room without eating anything. When her sister asked her if the pain was very bad, Anne replied quietly, "Yes, but it will soon be over." Still, the doctors did not seem worried, advising she be kept quiet and in bed. On the morning of the 27th, when the doctor arrived he found Anne in a coma. The diagnosis was meningitis.

The little patient returned to consciousness and extreme pain, although she remained uncomplaining and thankful for each little thing done for her comfort. She was given the last rites on December 30. On New Year's Day she seemed to rally, but was soon back fighting for breath. One day, near the end, she cried out excitedly, "JoJo, Leleine, Baby, come and see. Oh, look how beautiful it is!" The following day she told her mother that her guardian angel was there and insisted that her mother turn to see him. Later, when told the doctor was coming, Anne gently replied, "He can do nothing more for me."

A solemn face on a happy child

On the 14th of January, Anne turned to the nurse and asked, "Sister, may I go to the angels." As the nun bade her go, Anne replied softly, "Oh, thank you, thank you."

Her eyes were partially paralyzed so she could not raise them to the picture of Mary hanging on the wall of her room. Nonetheless, she quietly repeated the Hail Holy Queen. With a last effort, she lifted her eyelids for a final glance at her mother and then slipped quietly away.

Anne's frail little body was laid out on the bed in her room. After kneeling at her bedside for a long time, nine-year-old Jacques suddenly ran out of the room and began collecting everyone's prayer books and holy pictures. Returning, he piled them in a heap beside the bed and began pressing them, one by one, to Anne's hand. He told his astonished mother, "Some day you will be very glad I have done this."

A few days later, Anne's body was taken home to Annecy and laid in the family vault. Here, the people of the countryside who had known her remembered her as the little girl "who prays so well." Conversions and favors began to be reported through her intercession. In 1932, the Bishop of Annecy opened the canonical investigation into Anne's life and virtues. The ritual exhumation was set for October 30, 1933. Anne's body was found to be preserved intact at that time. She was reburied in a new casket in the same family vault. On March 3, 1990, Pope John Paul II approved the decree recognizing her heroic virtues. ✝

3

Annie Zelikova
Czechoslovakia, 1924–1942

Young Apostle of the Smile

Even as she lay dying from painful tuberculosis, Annie Zelikova was determined to continue smiling. She said, "I must smile to my last breath." Her beloved Jesus granted all that she asked of him: to do only with her as He willed. As she passed from this world, her face broke out with one of her beautiful smiles, and she whispered, "How beautiful ... it all is ... I wouldn't ... trade places ... with anyone. My heart ... is beating ... for Jesus. I love Him so much."

Annie Zelikova

Annie's own words give us the key to her happy heart: "We will show Him our love best if we wish only what he wishes, and are attentive to what makes Him happiest."

Although those who knew her already considered her a saint, the story of young Annie Zelikova was not known outside her region for over twenty years. It was not possible to initiate the process of her beatification until the break-down of the Communist regime. Today, Annie's smiling spirituality is spreading throughout the world and her cause for beatification is in Rome.

Annie's story is told in *Faces of Holiness II.* ✢

4

Blessed Antonia Mesina
Sardinia, 1919–1935

Catholic Action's Martyr for Purity

Annedda Castangia screamed and ran for help. Giovanni-Ignacio Catgui, a young man from town, had sneaked up behind her companion, Antonia, and when Antonia's attempts to break free failed, he had begun striking her with a rock. With his mind fixed on rape, Antonia's fierce defense of her purity turned the young man into a killing machine. Time and again he struck out in his rage.

Blessed Antonia Mesina

Breathless, Annedda arrived at the nearest house. The police were called, and, accompanied by a group of citizens, they returned to the woods to find the bloody and brutally murdered body of the sixteen-year-old Antonia. In his rage, Giovanni had struck her seventy-four times with the heavy rock. As Annedda sobbed out the murderer's name, she recalled that this bloody scene had only minutes before been the site of a tranquil discussion with Antonia about joining Catholic Action. Antonia had told her friend that membership in the group "is a beautiful experience and helps one to be good." Holding to her ideals until the end, Antonia had defended her purity even at the cost of her life.

Blessed Antonia in typical
Sardinian dress

Antonia Mesina was born June 21, 1919, in the small town of Orgosolo, high in the mountains of Sardinia. She was the second of ten children of a pious couple, Agostino and Grazia Raubanu Mesina. Augustino was a corporal in the cavalry that guarded the rural area around Orgosolo; Grazia was a devout housewife who attempted to bring her children up as good members of the Catholic Faith.

Antonia was baptized and confirmed shortly after her birth, according to the custom of the time. She was baptized at the age of nine days, and was confirmed the following year. As a young child, Antonia was lively, obedient and affectionate. Her teachers and classmates remember her as being well-liked, well-behaved, and studious. Antonia received her First Communion at the age of seven. At ten, she joined Catholic Action. She was a faithful member until the day of her death, and encouraged all her friends to join. Antonia always showed a generous attachment to her own family, and consideration and charity toward everyone.

During Antonia's fourth year of school, her mother developed a heart condition and was forbidden by the doctors to strain herself or lift anything heavy. Antonia was forced to leave school and take over many of the household duties. She helped with the cooking, the care of the children, the marketing, and the cleaning. The task of washing the family' clothes was hers alone, as her mother was not physically able to help with this chore. In the testimony for her beatification process, family and friends all testified that she worked cheerfully and diligently at her chores, and accepted the family's modest economic condition serenely. She was affectionate to the other children in the family and obedient to her parents. Her mother called her the "flower of my life."

Each week, Antonia baked bread for the family. This involved all parts of the process, including grinding the grain and gathering wood for the fire. On May 17, she had asked her friend Annedda to go with her to gather wood from the forest. On their walk, Antonia was discussing Catholic Action, trying to get Annedda to join the group. She pointed out that there were many spiritual benefits from the good works that the group performed. She also mentioned the catechetical instruction they received. When the girls had gathered enough wood, they were beginning the walk home when they noticed a teenage boy along the path. Annedda recognized him as a student at her school, but he turned off on a different path and the girls thought no more of him. Suddenly Antonia screamed for help. The boy had sneaked up behind them and grabbed Antonia, attempting to force her to the ground. She broke loose twice but was grabbed a third time and knocked down. The youth then began to strike her on the head and face with a large rock.

The relics of the young blessed are preserved in a wax image inside a glass casket

At first, Giovanni denied his guilt, attempting to hide his bloody clothes. Annedda had identified him, however, and two days later he confessed. He was tried and executed for his crime.

Antonia's remains were laid to rest in the local cemetery amid an outpouring of grief from all of the residents of her region. They soon began to pray to this humble young woman who chose a brutal death rather than dishonor. Later, her relics were transferred to a tomb in the Church of the Holy Savior. Antonia was beatified as a martyr for purity by Pope John Paul II on October 4, 1987. ✣

5

Charlene Marie Richard
United States, 1947-1959

A Cajun Saint?

Charlene Richard, a little Cajun girl, lived a simple life, strong in faith, in her rural home in Richard, Louisiana. A helpful child, Charlene was always eager to be of assistance to those around her. She had a quick wit, was an avid sports enthusiast, and was an active member of the Junior Catholic Daughters in her parish.

In 1959, Charlene was diagnosed with acute leukemia. She died just thirteen days later. During her last few days on earth, Charlene suffered terribly, but accepted her sufferings as God's will for her.

Young Charlene Richard

After her death, people began to ask Charlene's intercession for help over the rough spots in their lives. Just as she liked to be helpful in life, in death she seems to shower favors on those who ask in humble faith. Charlene's story has spread far outside the boundaries of southwest Louisiana. Many are drawn to the great gift this young Cajun girl has to offer: the example of child-like faith shown by her acceptance of God's will in her life.

At a commemorative Mass on the thirtieth anniversary of Charlene's death, Father Joseph Brennan, the hospital chaplain who attended her during her final illness, said, "Charlene taught us lessons in humility, acceptance, simplicity, and faith. We have many books teaching us how to live. Charlene wrote the book on how to die."

Charlene's story is detailed in *Faces of Holiness II.* ✢

6

Chiara Luce Badano
Italy, 1971–1990

Light for Unity

Conscious that the end of her life was very close, the young girl said, "Don't cry for me. I'm going to Jesus. At my funeral, I don't want people to cry; I want them to sing."

She planned her "wedding celebration," her funeral, with her mother. She wanted to be dressed like a bride, and she chose the music and the readings for the Mass. "While you're dressing me, Mom, you must repeat, 'Now Chiara Luce can see Jesus.'"

Nineteen-year-old Chiara Luce Badano was fully aware of her impending death of osteosarcoma with metastasis, one of the most serious and painful kinds of cancer. She wrote to Chiara Lubich, the founder of Focolare, "Medicine has quit the fight. Only God can do something now. Stopping the therapy means that the pain has increased in my back and I can hardly turn on my side anymore. Will I manage to be faithful to Jesus forsaken? I feel so small, and the road ahead seems so steep. I some-time feel suffocated by the pain. But it's my spouse who is coming to me, isn't it? I too want to repeat with you, 'If you want it, Jesus, I want it too.'"

A perky teen at age sixteen

Although Chiara wrote that she felt small, she knew the answer to this smallness. She wrote to two young friends, "Don't think you are too small! You aren't! What's important is that we say our 'yes' in the present moment. Living like this will make our unity even fuller, even more complete."

Chiara Badano followed her own advice and continuously said "yes." With her *fiat*, she began to realize the marvelous plan of God for her own life. She said, "Just as the doctors started this small but annoying procedure, a person came in to see me, a very beautiful lady with a luminous smile. She took my hand and encouraged me. Then she left. I don't know who she was, but I felt a very deep joy and all my fear disappeared. I realized that if we are always open to everything, God sends us many, many signs of His love."

Near the end of her life, it seemed to observers that she was already living in another world. At times, she asked her mother to leave her alone in the room. This was unusual, and she explained, "It doesn't mean that I don't love all of you or that I am sad. On the contrary. It's just hard to come down from where I was and then go back up." She explained to friends, "Another world was there for me, and I couldn't help but surrender myself. But now I feel enveloped in a marvelous plan of love that becomes always clearer to me."

———

Chiara Badano was born October 29, 1971, at Sassello, near Genoa, Italy. She was the only child of Ruggero Badano, a truck driver, and Maria Teresa Caviglia, a factory worker. They had hoped for a child all of the eleven years of their marriage, and were overjoyed when Chiara was born. Her mother stopped working to take care of her.

As she was the natural focus of attention from her parents and relatives, the Badanos tried hard not to spoil her. Once, while still quite young, Chiara came home with an apple she had taken without permission from their neighbor's fruit stand. When her mother told her she had to return it, and apologize to their neighbor, the young child balked. She was ashamed and embarrassed because of what she had done. Her mother impressed on her that telling the truth was much more important than the apple, so Chiara went and made her apology. That evening the neighbor brought over a basket of apples for Chiara since she had "learned a very important lesson."

Chiara – "Little Miss Sunshine"

Chiara was naturally generous and giving. On a first-grade writing assignment, she wrote a letter to the Baby Jesus. Instead of asking for toys for herself, she asked, "Please make Grandma get well, and all those who are sick."

Chiara had a soft spot for the sick and the elderly and always tried to help them. In one entry of Chiara's diary we read, "One of my classmates has scarlet fever and the other students are afraid to go visit her. With the approval of my parents, I'll go tomorrow to bring her the school assignments so she won't feel alone."

As with all normal children, she sometimes quarreled with her parents, but the differences were rare and didn't last long. Once she refused to help her mother clear the table after supper and went to her room instead. In a few moments she returned and reminded her mother of the Gospel tale of the two laborers in the vineyard — one said "yes" and didn't go and the other said "no" but then went. "Mom, give me my apron," she said as she began to take care of the table.

First Communion

At nine, Chiara came into contact with the ideal of unity during a meeting of the youth of the Focolare. This had a profound effect on her life. A few years later, she wrote, "I discovered that Jesus forsaken is the key to unity with God, and I want to choose him as my only spouse. I want to be ready to welcome him when he comes. To prefer him above all else."

Chiara's parents met the Focolare in 1981 at a large gathering for families. The Focolare is a worldwide ecumenical movement. It came into being during World War II, when Chiara Lubich and a group of young women resolved to live as persons whose actions and thoughts would be based on the Gospel. The spirituality that developed was to be a spirituality of unity, a way to go to God together. Afterwards, her mother says, "when someone asked us when we got married, we used to say when we met this way of life!"

As a teenager, Chiara was a beautiful girl with delicate features, large, limpid eyes, and lustrous dark hair. During her final illness, the archbishop of her city came to visit her and asked her where the light in her eyes came from. She responded, "I try to love Jesus a lot."

Otherwise, her teen years were much like those of other girls her age. Her parents moved to a larger town, Savona, to allow her to go to high school. Here she was very popular and participated in tennis, swimming, and hiking. She dressed well, although not extravagantly, and loved to sing and dance. She liked to stay out late at night with her friends, "hanging out" at the coffee shop. After a few disagreements, she and her parents came to a compromise about her curfew time. She developed a special friendship with a boy named Luke, but eventually broke it off. Although she had friendships with other boys, none of them were serious.

Chiara failed her first year of high school, and this caused her a lot of pain. In the summer of 1988, she needed to study because she hadn't done well in math, but she had promised to accompany some of the youngest Focolare children, ages four to nine, to a congress in Rome. She honored her promise, and from Rome she wrote her parents, "Something very important happened here; I encountered Jesus crucified and forsaken. It has not been easy for me to love Him in my suffering, but this morning Chiara Lubich explained to the Gen 4 (the name of the Focolare group) that He has to be the spouse of our soul."

Following this trip, she began to correspond with Chiara Lubich, and asked her for a new name that would signify her new life. The foundress answered her, "Chiara Luce" — Chiara Light.

One day, while playing tennis, Chiara felt a severe pain in her shoulder. At first she ignored it, but eventually tests determined that she was suffering from cancer. Even in the hospital, she was noted for her attitude of self-giving. She helped one depressed young drug addict by accompanying her at any time she was needed, even when getting up caused Chiara strong pain in her back. "Later, I'll have time to rest," she said. In spite of her illness, Chiara continued to try and live a joyful life.

Chiara underwent two painful operations and chemotherapy. She lost her

Chiara with the youngest Focolare group, the Gen 4

hair, and the disease began to ravage her body, although her eyes remained bright and beautiful. One day, she gave all her savings to a friend who was leaving to do missionary work in Africa. She told him, "I don't need this money anymore. I have everything."

Eventually, Chiara became unable to walk. She said, "If I had to choose between walking again and going to heaven, I wouldn't hesitate. I would choose heaven." She refused morphine saying, "I want to stay clear-headed because the only thing I can do is offer this pain to Jesus. I still want to share a little bit of His cross with Him." On one of her last days, she said, "I'm not asking Jesus to come and take me to heaven with Him. I don't want him to get the impression that I don't want to suffer for Him anymore."

She told her mother, "Oh Mamma, young people ... young people ... they are the future. You see, I can't run anymore, but how I would like to pass on to them the torch, like in the Olympics! Young people have only one life, and it's worthwhile to spend it well."

One of her doctors wrote to her, "I am not used to seeing young people like you. . . . You've taught me that young people can also show great maturity."

On October 7, 1990, Chiara went to meet her Spouse. Her parents were next to her, and friends were outside the door. Her last words were for her mother, "Bye, Mom, be happy because I'm very happy." Chiara Luce — Chiara Light — lived up to the promise of her new name. Through the light of Christ crucified and forsaken, Chiara Luce has become a beacon of holiness for modern teens.

The process of beatification for the Servant of God Chiara Badano has been opened and is being studied in Rome. ✝

7

Danny George
United States, 1991–1996

Giving the Love and Peace of Jesus

The rays of the bright Texas sun fell on the bed of four-year-old Danny George, who was suffering the painful agony of the leukemia which had plagued him since his first year. In anguish, his Uncle Luke sat beside the dying boy and explained that he needed to return to Wyoming because he needed to help his father. In reality, it was the pain of watching Danny's terrible suffering that Luke could not bear. As Danny watched his beloved uncle, his best buddy, leave to pack, he asked his mother "Why is Luke leaving, Mama?"

Susan George told her son the truth: "It is very difficult for Uncle Luke to see you suffer, Danny. It is too painful for him to bear without his Dad here with him so he needs to go home to Grandpa now."

Danny's look at his mother showed he understood, but was still ineffably sad. Later, Luke came in the bedroom where Susan was reading to her son. After a few moments, Luke got tears in his eyes and he left the room quickly. Danny asked his Mom why Luke was crying and she explained that it was because of the struggle he was having because of his love for Danny and his fear of seeing Danny suffer. Danny closed his eyes in prayer. When he opened them again, they were filled with joy and peace. "I know what I'm going to do. I'm going to give Uncle Luke the love and peace of Jesus that is in my heart so he won't be sad any more." His face lit up at the thought of the gift he would give his best buddy.

When Luke returned, Danny whispered to his mother, "Tell him, Mama, what I'm going to do for him." Luke received this gift with joy, and says that from that moment on he was filled with a great peace.

Jesus said, "I came that they may have life, and have it abundantly" (John 10:10). Although Danny George lived a brief life, it was abundant in the love of God. At his tender age, he knew and lived the words: "And this is eternal life, that they may know thee the only true God, and Jesus Christ whom thou hast sent" (John 17:3).

———

Danny was born November 10, 1991, at home in Powell, Wyoming. His father, Tom, took the newborn infant into the chapel of the Catholic student center which they ran. The chapel was between their home and the student center where they worked. Tom consecrated baby Danny to Our Lord in the Eucharist. From that moment, it seemed as if the Eucharistic Lord began to accompany and to infuse the child with a special grace, as the child, through his suffering, seemed to join in the Paschal mystery.

Shortly after Danny's birth, his family decided to serve the Church as lay apostles in the Society of Our Lady of the Most Holy Trinity. The society, commonly known as SOLT, was founded by Father James Flanagan on July 16, 1958. It consists of priests, religious brothers and sisters, deacons, and both married and single lay people. SOLT's charism is the discipleship of Mary and Jesus in ecclesial teams of priests, brothers, sisters, and laity — and Marian-Trinitarian spirituality in the areas of deepest apostolic need.

The George family moved to Skidmore, Texas, for a year of formation, after which they returned to Wyoming, where Danny's apostolate of suffering began. On May 29, 1993, Danny was diagnosed with Acute Lymphoblastic Leukemia. He was in critical condition. Fortunately, Father Tony Anderson, one of the SOLT priests, had just arrived in town. He anointed Danny, and then lent them a van to drive immediately to the children's hospital in Denver. After two weeks, Danny's disease was in remission, but there was a great deal of pain from the side effects of the chemotherapy, and he was plagued with secondary infections.

In 1995, Danny relapsed; the leukemia had affected his bone marrow. On hearing the news, his parents and two older sisters broke down. Immersed in pain, Danny told his mother not to cry and tried to comfort "his girls."

The Georges had two options: a bone marrow transplant, where Danny would have only a twenty to thirty percent chance of survival, or taking Danny to the American Metabolic Institute in Tijuana, Mexico. This institute has had success with cancer patients who have no hope with traditional medicine. The big obstacle to the Mexico clinic was that Danny's medical coverage would not pay for it. The Georges asked for Father Flanagan's advice, and he counseled that unless they were given the money to begin Danny's treatment, they should take him to Denver. Susan was pregnant with her fifth child and due in a few weeks. The realities of life and death were pressing on the family. With no hope of funding the Mexico trip, the family was just walking out the door to go to Denver when a friend called and offered to give the Georges the $24,000 which Danny's treatment in Mexico would cost.

As the family left, they stopped to see Father Kevin Koche, pastor of Saint Joseph's Church in Lovell, Wyoming. Father Kevin gave Danny the anointing of the sick, and the family left for Mexico with a friend and her son who planned to help with the birth of the baby and the care of the children.

Only a few miles from town, the transmission went out on the van. The Georges were able to schedule a flight for Tom and Danny for the following morning, and since they would have to stay in Lovell that night, the family attended Mass at Saint Joseph's. Father Kevin offered the Mass for Danny and told the congregation what had happened.

After Mass, Father Kevin came and sat by the family; his eyes were filled with tears. He told them that as they drove off, Our Lord called out to him to give Danny his First Communion and to confirm him. (He had been designated by the bishop to give both sacraments in a pilot program.) Since the family had driven off, Father believed Our Lord's request was impossible, so he prayed, "If you want this done, Jesus, then bring the George family back here." Father Kevin then asked for the privilege of giving three-year-old Danny these sacraments of the Church.

After questioning Danny, Father Kevin gave him the sacraments; he also served as Danny's confirmation sponsor. Immediately after receiving the sacraments, Danny got down from his mother's lap and began to walk. He hadn't been able to walk for two weeks because of the severe pain in his legs. Danny said, "Mama, I want to go play with the other kids now." The entire family rejoiced in the gift of grace and strength which lasted for about five hours. The following day, Tom and Danny flew to Mexico.

Three weeks later, Susan gave birth to Theresa Lillian Marie. A few days later, Susan, the baby, and a friend left for Mexico to relieve Tom. His job was on the line, and he needed to return to work. So when Susan arrived, Tom went back to work in Wyoming.

In the meantime, Danny was making slow but steady progress. A Eucharistic minister brought Danny Communion almost every day, and the Eucharistic Lord was his strength.

In spite of all the painful procedures, both in Mexico and later at home, Danny never became bitter or angry at the doctors and nurses. In Mexico, Dr. Rubio told Danny, "You are my best patient. I must have you teach the grown-ups here how to be a good patient and do all that is asked of them so they can get well."

Danny George
1991-1996

On the night of November 7, Tom was late calling Susan for his daily check on Danny's progress. Danny was not doing well; he still had fifty percent leukemia cells in his bone marrow. Tom's voice was shaky. There had been a serious accident, caused by a flat tire, involving three trucks with trailers. The accident involved Bishoff Ranch employees, all friends and relatives of the Georges. One child, Veronica, was the only one seriously hurt. She had been pinned in the door of one of the trucks when another hit it, and was in serious condition. She was being consoled by her mother as they awaited the arrival of the ambulance, and her mother asked Veronica if she wanted to offer her pain up as a sacrifice for someone. She yelled out, "for Danny," and kept saying that as she prayed Hail Marys. Veronica was rushed to the hospital with her brother, who had received a sharp bump on his head.

Our Lord accepted Veronica's offering, and the next day there were no leukemia cells in his bone marrow. Danny was in complete remission. He was able to leave the hospital on his birthday,

November 10, 1995. His best birthday present was to be reunited with his family in Wyoming.

Within only a few weeks, Danny was feeling pain in his legs again and could not walk. His white-cell count was up, indicating an infection, but no sign that the leukemia had returned. On the night of December 12, the family was able to host a visit of the Missionary Image of Our Lady of Guadalupe. Danny was entranced with the image and told his sisters, "Girls, look at Mary, my Mother." For the first time in weeks, Danny slept peacefully and without pain. The next day, Danny could walk again for the first time in two weeks. He played with his sisters and enjoyed his last Christmas on earth with his family. He had begun to forge an even deeper love and relationship with Our Lady, and from that time on he always referred to Mary as "My Mother." As he informed his mother, "You are my Mama, Mary is my Mother."

Daily, in his pain, Danny grew closer to the crucified Lord, who gave this child many gifts of grace and wisdom. Anyone who has ever intimately known a four or five-year-old child can tell you that occasionally they will astound you with a remark whose truth and wisdom is beyond their years. Hence the trite but very true saying, "Out of the mouths of babes." The depth of some of Danny's remarks often startled his parents and those serving him. Danny, who had remained a daily communicant, seemed infused with a holy wisdom and often seems to have been given mystical graces. One night when the pain was extremely severe, Danny was crying out. A while later, he seemed to improve drastically and had a kind of supernatural peace about him. When his father asked him if something had happened, Danny replied, "My Mother helped me."

Another time, when his mother was sleeping with him in the hospital, she awoke to hear him cry out, "Mother." Trying to soothe him, she said, "I'm right here, Danny, Mama is with you." The child replied, "Not you, Mama, her!" He returned to staring at a spot by his bed. He kept calling out, every so often, "Mother, Mother." A few minutes later, Tom and Father Jim came into the room. Tom walked up to the bed-rail where Danny had been looking at "her." Danny cried out, "Daddy, you made her leave. Go get her." Tom looked puzzled, but Susan whispered that they had a visitor that she couldn't see but whom Danny could see. Danny asked his father to go and look for her in the hall. When asked what she looked like, Danny just said she had on white and blue and again begged his father to go into the hall to find her. He seemed disappointed when Tom didn't return with his visitor.

The following day, when Susan asked who she was, Danny replied that it was his Mother. Asked if she said anything, the boy replied, "No, she just smiled at me and comforted me and gave me strength."

In April, Danny underwent a bone-marrow transplant at the University of Minnesota hospital. His sister, Bridgette, was a perfect match and was his donor. The next months were a roller-coaster ride with many ups and downs.

One day, Tom teasingly asked Danny if he would be his spiritual director. When Danny replied, "Sure, Daddy," his father asked him what he needed to do to become a saint. Danny answered immediately, "Believe in Jesus and love Mama with your whole heart." When the Georges shared this four-year-old's wisdom with Father Flanagan, he laughed joyously and said, "What do you need me for, then?"

In June, the family joyfully returned to Wyoming for a brief reunion with family and friends and then moved to Corpus Christi, Texas, to be with the family of Our Lady's Society. They were welcomed to Trinity House, a dwelling where Danny could spend the last days of his life with his family.

Some cousins had come to visit when the family was at the hospital in Minnesota for the bone-marrow transplant. They took the girls to swim in the pool at the hotel. Wistfully, Danny expressed the wish that he also could go for a swim. Susan says that is the only time she recalls Danny ever saying anything about what the other children were doing that he couldn't do. He seems to have been given a particular grace to have never been bitter, resentful, or jealous of the things the other children could do. He accepted his crosses of pain and immobility with serenity and peace, never complaining or pitying himself because of his illness.

When the family arrived at Trinity House, the first thing Danny noticed was the pool. "Look! Mary, my Mother, gave us a pool to swim in!" he cried joyously. The pool was great physical therapy for Danny, and his health was better than it had been since he was a baby. The family was overjoyed to see him run and play with his sisters. In many ways, Danny was still very much a normal little boy. Although he had apparently been given mystical graces, Danny loved to roughhouse and play with his sisters and his parents. He teased and laughed as any happy little boy his age would do.

Nightly, Danny was hooked up to the Kangaroo Pump, which fed him through a gastric tube in his stomach. During these times, he and his mother had long conversations, and she was amazed at his relationship with Our Lady and the Trinity, which he detailed to her. At one point, he recalled to her a time he nearly died while in the hospital at Billings, Montana. "I was drowning, Mama, but it wasn't in water. Everything was black and I couldn't breathe. Then my Mother came and she picked me up in her arms and I could breathe again. She had white around her hair and a red dress on."

A few days later, on a visit to Robstown, Danny and Susan were in the chapel of San Jose House. Danny found a book of the SOLT spiritual exercises. Excitedly, he showed his mother a picture of Our Lady of the Trinity, telling her that this was what his Mother looked like. When Susan asked if Danny's mother had the symbol of the Trinity as shown in the picture, he eagerly replied yes, but that there was a little fire of red and yellow around the symbol. Just as Danny saw her, she had a white veil on her hair, but he said that her dress was red, not blue as shown in the picture. Susan obtained another copy of the book and colored it with markers as Danny described his Mother. The picture became Danny's favorite thing, and he put it under his pillow each night when he went to bed.

One evening at supper, the family was sharing the things they were most thankful for. Danny commented that he was "thankful to be here and for Jesus giving me His Body and Blood." In Danny's simple comment, there was a profound knowledge and depth of gratitude for the gift of life.

Sadly, Danny's leukemia soon returned with a vengeance. The doctors confirmed that medically there was nothing more they could do. The Georges could keep him in the hospital, and chemotherapy might prolong his life a few months, or they could take him home and give him hospice care.

After hearing the news, the family was crying when Danny came back into the room. Calmly, Danny said, "I know why you are crying, Mama. My leukemia is back."

She sobbed out, "Yes, Danny; what do we do now?"

He took her hand as if to comfort her and answered, "We need to trust in Jesus. And we shall call Father Flanagan and ask him to meet us at San Jose House to give me Jesus." What wisdom sprang from this little child as he linked the reality of his terminal disease with the Paschal mystery of Christ in the Eucharist.

Danny's parents agreed to allow Danny to make the decision as to what to do. They carefully explained what the doctors had said. Wanting to make certain he understood, his father told him, "Danny, the doctors have told us that there is nothing left they can do to stop your leukemia. They say that you will die from it. Do you know what dying means, Danny?"

With a calm certainty, Danny replied, "Yes, Daddy, it is Jesus on the cross." Without hesitation, Danny chose to stay at home with his family at Trinity House.

During his final days, Danny relapsed into the pain so familiar in his short life. He was blessed with the visits of friends, relatives, and the members of Our Lady's Society. A number of the health-care personnel assigned to him say they were drawn to his room like a magnet; because of his peace and joy, they came to have their spirits lifted. When his mother wanted to give him some pain medication, for the first time he refused to do what he was asked. Danny wanted to give all his suffering to Jesus, seeking no relief.

Danny continued to receive Communion daily, and often the priests of SOLT would come and say Mass in the living room at Trinity House. After receiving, Danny would fall back on his pillow and close his eyes. Once, his sister Elizabeth asked him if he was all right during one of these times. "Shh, Lizzy, I'm praying to Jesus," he chided her.

At one point as he neared his final days, he found his mother crying. Consoling her, he held her. Then she heard him whisper as if talking to himself, "I have a job to do. I'll ask Jesus if He will do it for me so I can be with Mama a little longer."

Danny seemed to get a little better, so one morning Tom asked his son, "Danny, did you ask Jesus to heal you?" Danny nodded in the affirmative, so Tom asked, "What did Jesus say about it?"

Danny responded, "He was going to talk to Mary about it."

Tom continued, "So Mary can heal you?"

Looking at his father as if he felt his father had just said something quite foolish, Danny replied, "No, Dad. Jesus is the healer. He just wanted to talk to his Mother about it."

Asked by his grandmother if his Mother Mary had visited him, Danny replied that she had, but would not talk about what she said. Later he told his mother that some devils had been bothering him and asked for Father Flanagan to come and hear his confession. Later, Danny surprised his mother by asking where Saint Michael got his beautiful sword, and telling her that it was powerful and killed all the devils. Susan didn't remember ever talking to Danny about Saint Michael and could only suppose he had seen the statue at one of the SOLT houses.

Danny died in the presence of both his parents on November 7, 1996. Father Tony came in the room and blessed him as his soul winged its way to Jesus and His Mother.

Father Flanagan was in Mexico, and he left on a bus immediately. After forty-two hours on the bus, Father came and prayed beside Danny's casket, giving thanks for Danny's life and his death in Christ. Then he shared a precious story with Tom and Susan.

The morning of Danny's death, an older girl who had been selling herself on the streets in Colon, had taken two younger girls and left the orphanage. Once Father Flanagan learned that Danny had been taken home, he prayed to Danny and asked his help to bring the girls back to the orphanage. Sister Mary Teresa, in charge of the orphanage, had also asked Danny's help. The girls were then found very quickly and returned to the orphanage safe and sound. Father Jim felt interiorly that Danny had heard his request and gone right to work to obtain that grace.

Danny was buried in Immaculate Conception Cemetery in Skidmore, Texas. Members of Our Lady's Society and others whose lives Danny touched during his own brief stay on earth often visit. An image of his Mother, Our Lady of the Trinity, adorns the marker over his tiny grave.

Shortly after Danny's death, his parents were sent to build a lay formation center for Our Lady's Society in Florida. Unknown to their parents, Bridgett and Elizabeth began asking Danny in prayer every day to go to Jesus and obtain a new baby for the family. The work of building was going rapidly when Susan began to feel sick. She was just ready to go and see a doctor when she realized what was happening. A test confirmed that the family was going to be blessed with another child. Michael Joseph Daniel George was born October 2, 1997.

"The LORD gave, and the LORD has taken away; blessed be the name of the LORD" (Job 1:21). ✣

8

Saint Dominic Savio
Italy, 1842–1857

Saintly Student

Dominic Savio decided to become a saint. Immediately he went to the chapel to pray. He refused to play any games with the other boys and put on a long, serious face. For two days Dominic remained in this sober attitude. Finally, Don Bosco, his teacher, called to him, asking if he felt sick. Dominic assured him that he felt particularly well and happy. Then why, asked Don Bosco, had Dominic refused to play his customary games, and why the sober expression?

When Dominic explained his great desire to become a saint, Don Bosco praised his decision but counseled him to be cheerful, and not to worry; serving God is the way to true happiness. "Enjoy yourself as much as you like if only you keep from sin."

———

Dominic was born on April 2, 1842, the son of a very poor blacksmith in the little town of Castelnuovo d'Asti. His parents, Charles and Brigid, were warm and loving and attempted in every way to bring their son up as a good Christian.

From the time he was a small child, Dominic was attracted to all things religious. He begged to help the priest at Mass when he was only five. More than simply observing religious customs and practices, however, Dominic lived his religion for the entire span of his brief life.

In Dominic's day, children normally did not make First Communion until they were about eleven or twelve years old. Dominic was filled with a great desire to receive Jesus, and after consultation with some other priests who saw the maturity of this small boy, his parish priest allowed him to make his First Communion at the age of seven. Later, Dominic always said, " That was the happiest and most wonderful day of my life." He made some promises that day and wrote them in a little book which he often re-read, and which were the guiding light of his life.

He wrote:

Promises made by me, Dominic Savio, when I made my First Communion at the age of seven years:

1. I will go often to Confession, and I will go to Holy Communion as often as I am allowed.
2. I will try to give the Sundays and holy days completely to God.
3. My best friends will be Jesus and Mary.
4. Death, but not sin.

Dominic attended the small school in his village and after a few years he walked a six-mile round trip daily to attend a larger school in a nearby town.

One day, while the teacher was out of the room, two boys brought in a lot of snow and trash and stuffed it into the only iron stove, which was heating the room. When the teacher returned, he was so angry that the two guilty boys claimed that Dominic had done it. The teacher gave Dominic a severe scolding, telling him that were this not his first offense, he would have been immediately expelled. Dominic said not one word in his own defense, but stood in front of the class and hung his head while the teacher scolded.

The next day some of the other boys probably tattled. At any rate, the teacher learned the truth of the matter. He went immediately to Dominic and asked why he had not answered the charges made against him. Dominic said that he knew the teacher would have expelled the other boys, and he wanted them to have another chance. "Besides," said Dominic, "I remembered that Our Lord was unjustly accused and He said nothing." Even at this early age, Dominic had begun the practice of the virtue which was later declared heroic at his beatification.

In 1854, Don Cugliero, Dominic's teacher, went to Turin and spoke with the great Saint John Bosco, asking him to admit Dominic to the Oratory. A meeting was arranged, and after a brief interview Don Bosco was very favorably impressed. He later wrote, "I recognized in him a soul where the Holy Spirit reigned supreme, and I marveled at the way grace had already worked in his young heart and mind."

Just as Don Bosco was going to call Dominic's father over, the boy said, "Well, Father, what do you think? Will you take me to Turin to study?"

"Well, I think there is good stuff in you."

"Good stuff for what?"

"To make a beautiful garment for Our Blessed Lord."

"Wonderful! I am the cloth and you are the tailor. You will work on me and make something beautiful for Jesus."

So Dominic went to Turin and became a pupil at Don Bosco's Oratory. There he worked, studied, played, and prayed for three years before his final illness forced him to return home.

During Dominic's brief time at the Oratory, he gained the love and respect of all the boys and the priests. He was not pushy and would not interrupt to state his own views, but he was not afraid to oppose wrong and could always give reasons why he thought a certain action was wrong. Best of all, Dominic had taken to heart and internalized Don Bosco's advice: "Enjoy yourself as much as you like, if only you keep from sin." Dominic's love of God was displayed in his genuinely cheerful and joyous attitude.

One day, as Dominic was getting acquainted with a newcomer to the Oratory, he explained to the boy, "Here we make holiness consist in living as joyfully as we can. We take care to avoid sin — that great thief which robs us of the grace of God and peace of soul; we neglect no duty and so seek God with all our hearts. Begin from now and take as your motto these words: 'Serve the Lord with holy joy.'"

Once, Dominic overheard two boys planning a rock fight. They had become very angry with each other and were going to fight it out. Dominic tried his best to talk them out of the dangerous idea, but nothing would sway their determination. He could have told the teacher, but he felt this would only have served to postpone the fight. Finally, he made the boys agree to one secret condition, which he would tell them about just before the fight. The morning of the fight, Dominic went with the boys and helped them make their preparations by piling up rocks. When the boys were ready to begin, Dominic held up a small crucifix and reminded them that Christ died forgiving sins, but that they were going to fight a dangerous fight to get even for a minor slight. "Now," said Dominic, "throw your first rock at me. That is my condition."

At this demand, one of the boys said, "But Dominic, you have never hurt me or done anything to me, and you are my friend."

"You will not hurt me, a poor human, but will you, by your actions, hurt Jesus Christ who is also God?" asked Dominic.

The boys hung their heads in shame and dropped their stones. Dominic never mentioned this incident, and we would have no record of it had not the two combatants told all their friends.

Dominic had a great love for the Mother of God, and organized a club, the Company of Mary Immaculate, to honor her. His stories of the Blessed Mother were a favorite entertainment with the younger boys. One May, the boys in his dormitory decided to put up a little altar to Mary and had a meeting to decide what each one should give. At the meeting, Dominic was one of the most enthusiastic about the project, but realized he had no money to contribute for his share. After thinking a moment, he returned to his room and came back with a nice book which he had won as a prize. He told his companions to raffle it off to gain the money needed for the supplies for the altar. Inspired by his generosity, several of the others contributed little treasures of their own and a successful raffle was held so that all the required materials could be bought.

A common representation of the young saint

One special friend of Dominic's was another student named John Massaglia, who, like Dominic, was from a neighboring country parish and who also wanted to be a priest. They were good companions in the Company of Mary Immaculate and once, on retreat, each took a vow to help the other grow in virtue and to be anxious for the welfare of each other's soul.

At the first of the school year in 1857, John's health failed and his parents took him home to rest. He wrote to Dominic asking him to send some books and notes he had left in Turin. In Dominic's reply, he wrote, "You say you don't know if you will ever come back to the Oratory. To tell you the truth, I have a feeling that I am coming quickly to the end of my own life. At any rate we can pray for each other so that both of us may die happily in God's grace. The one who goes to heaven first can prepare a place for the other and, when he arrives, stretch out a helping hand to pull him in! May God keep us always in His holy grace and help us to become saints, but quickly because there is little time left. All your friends look forward to your coming back and send their very best wishes. With theirs, I send you my own best wishes and prayers."

A short time afterward, John passed away peacefully after receiving the last sacraments. Although he accepted it as God's will, Dominic was deeply grieved by his friend's death. He never forgot John in his prayers right up to the time of his own death, a few short months afterwards.

Dominic was apparently favored with a number of mystical gifts. The innocence of his life, his love of God and his great desire for the things of God so developed Dominic's mind that he came to be habitually united with God. As he told Don Bosco, "It is silly of me, I get a distraction and lose the thread of my prayers and then I see such wonderful things that the hours pass by like minutes." In one of his "distractions," he remained standing, gazing at the tabernacle an entire morning until the rector who had missed him from class and lunch found him and shook him back to consciousness. Sometimes this happened during class or recreation, and he would pass out from the beauty of the sights he was seeing. Once he gave Don Bosco a message for the Pope which he had seen in a vision.

Another time he burst into the saint's room crying out, "Come quickly! There is good work to be done." Don Bosco followed Dominic through the winding streets of Turin to a house and at their knock the woman flung open the door with an enthusiastic welcome, begging them to hurry to the side of her dying husband. He was a lapsed Catholic, and Don Bosco was able to give him the last sacraments only a few moments before he died. When Don Bosco asked Dominic how he knew the man was dying, Dominic looked at the saint somewhat sadly and burst into tears. Don Bosco did not question him further.

Few who lived with him were aware of Dominic's mystical gifts. They saw only a very cheerful, normal, and exceptionally good boy.

Much of his life was hidden until Don Bosco wrote about him after his death.

Never in robust health, Dominic became quite ill in the spring of 1857. He took his sad and solemn farewell from the Oratory on March 1. He had begged to be allowed to stay, but Don Bosco felt it was best that he return to his parents.

At home, he first seemed to improve. The local doctor diagnosed an inflammation of the lungs. The treatment in those days consisted of bloodletting, or slitting a vein and letting "excess" blood drain out. In the space of four days, the doctor cut Dominic's arm ten times. Far from helping, this probably hastened his death. Although he seemed to be better, Dominic asked for the last sacraments, which were brought to him. He died quietly in his home that evening, March 9, 1857. His last words were, "Oh, what wonderful things I see."

Don Bosco and the boys at the Oratory had been anxiously awaiting word of Dominic. His father's letter arrived; it began, "With my heart full of grief I send you this sad news. Dominic, my dear son and your child in God, gave his soul to God on March 9th, after having received with the greatest devotion the last sacraments and the papal blessing."

Two photos of Saint John Bosco with the boys of his Oratory. We do not know if Dominic is in the group, but the photos show how the boys of Dominic's time dressed

Dominic's friends were the first to realize his sanctity. They began praying to him, and soon reports of a cured toothache or a passing mark on an exam were brought to Don Bosco. In 1876, Dominic appeared to Don Bosco in one of the saint's vivid dreams. At this time he made several predictions, and when asked, told Don Bosco that he was in heaven. Dominic himself was beautiful and glorious, and he appeared in the company of many other blessed souls.

"The Oratory has had many saintly boys, some of whom have practiced virtue as heroically as Saint Aloysius." These words of Don Bosco were certainly true in the case of Dominic Savio. Dominic was beatified in 1950 and canonized in 1954. Pope Saint Plus X called Dominic a true model for the youth of our times. Dominic lived the type of life that can be imitated by teenagers all over the world. It is fitting that the two miracles accepted for his beatification involved teenagers. ✢

9

Ellen Organ
Ireland, 1903–1908

Little Nellie of Holy God

Four-year-old Nellie Organ looked at the statue of Our Lady holding the Christ Child. She reached out and touched the globe which the infant held. Winsomely, she said, "Give me your ball and I will give you my shoes."

"Oh Nellie," the nurse immediately responded, "you can't get that."

Passing on, Nellie replied confidently, "He can give 'em if he likes."

Merely a childish fancy? Yes. But also a prime example of the childlike faith that Our Lord told us we all need to get to heaven: "Let the children come to me, and do not hinder them; for to such belongs the kingdom of God. Truly, I say to you, whoever does not receive the kingdom of God like a child shall not enter it" (Luke 18:16-17). It is also an indicator of the grace that can work in the soul of even the youngest of God's children.

The grace of a solid, undisturbed faith in the one she always called "Holy God" was a hallmark of the life of Ellen Organ, a little Irish girl who died in the odor of sanctity at the age of four and a half. Nellie displayed heroic fortitude in suffering from the consumptive tuberculosis that took her life. While those who loved her wept at the pathetic sight, she remained happy and resigned, chastising one by saying, "Why are you crying, Mother? You should be happy I am going to Holy God." At the last, another told her that the more patient she was in suffering the closer she would be to Him afterwards, and Nellie confidently responded, "But I will fly to Him!" Then she calmly told them that she would go to Holy God on His own day, wearing her First Communion dress and in the arms of her beloved nurse. She told them to make a dress for Nurse, and then lay back in joyful anticipation of her flight.

———

Ellen Organ was born in the family quarters of the Royal Garrison Artillery Barracks in the town of Waterford on August 24, 1903. She was the last of the four children of William and Mary Organ. Just as they had with their older children, the pious couple took baby Ellen, whom they called Nellie, to be baptized at the parish church, Holy Trinity, within a few days after her birth. Although not blessed with the things of this earth, the family was rich in their faith and love, and spent two happy years here. Later, her father would recall of Nellie, "When she was two, she would clasp my hand and toddle off to Mass at 'Trinity Without' (the eccentric nickname for the parish church), prattling all the way about Holy God."

After two years in Waterford, Private Organ was transferred to a small island fort in Cork harbor called Spike. Mary already had tuberculosis and succumbed to the damp climate of Cork Harbor, dying in 1907 when Nellie was three years old. The child had to be torn from her mother's dying embrace and from that point on always referred to Mary as "dead mother."

Alone, William could not care for his children, and the local priest made arrangements for the children at the charitable institutions of the diocese. Thomas, the oldest, was sent to the school of the Brothers of Charity at Upton; David went to the convent school of the Sisters of Mercy at Passage West. The two girls, Mary and Nellie, were sent to the Industrial School of the Good Shepherd Sisters at Sunday's Well. When William eventually retired from the Army, he moved back to his hometown of Dungarvan, married again, and had two more children.

Mary and Nellie arrived at the Good Shepherd Convent in May of 1907. The resident nurse, Miss Hall, found that both had whooping cough, so the children were in hospital for the first days of their stay. Nellie's generosity to others was noted from this first meeting. She had been crying from the pain of the cough that wracked her little frame, and the nurse gave her some sweet candies to soothe her throat. Smiling through her tears, Nellie insisted that Nurse Hall and her sister share the treats before taking any for herself.

The children were released from the hospital in July and returned to Sunday's Well. The whooping cough had been cured, but the children still looked delicate and frail. Although Mary eventually recovered her health, the next eight months before her early death were to be ones of extraordinary suffering for Nellie. Most of the time she was nearly bedridden, at first in the infirmary of the school and later in the room of the resident nurse, Miss Hall, an admirable young woman and recent convert to the Faith who loved Nellie with the tender care of a surrogate mother. Nellie suffered from the same form of wasting tuberculosis that had killed her mother. In addition, she suffered from a severe spinal problem and, later, severe caries which caused her jawbone to crumble. During these brief months, grace operated in the soul of this youngest of believers and led her to a degree of sanctity which many people hope will one day lead to a cause for her beatification.

On Nellie's first Sunday with the sisters, because of the feast of Saint Mary Magdalen, the community's patron, special music was presented for the Mass in the sisters' chapel. Nellie spent the majority of time at Mass turned backwards in her place, looking up at the organist and choir with her large brown eyes. She was passionately fond of music, and all her biographers mention that she often made up and sang happy little songs during her days at Sunday's Well.

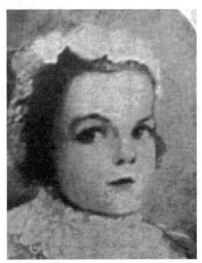

Little Nellie in her First Communion veil

At first, although Nellie's intelligence and her affectionate and generous nature were observed, some thought she was also a bit peevish and self-willed as she frequently fell into tears, especially when told to sit still. She was scolded for this, and thereafter attempted to control her tears and not complain. It wasn't until a girl who slept next to her in the dormitory mentioned that Nellie cried all night that it was discovered her spine was extremely curved, which must have caused her a great deal of pain, especially when sitting. After this, she was sent to the infirmary where she could have constant attention. Here, she was able to take her breakfast in bed instead of going to eat with the other children. She usually shared it with a small black kitten which she was extremely fond of.

Although she seemed especially favored, Nellie was still a little girl. Just like all little girls, she got into a few childish scrapes. Once she nearly choked to death on some beads she had been given to play with which she put into her mouth. Another time she squeezed her beloved little kitten so tightly as to endanger the little animal's breathing. She wasn't always perfectly behaved, but her contrition for her little faults was immediate and genuine. Once, thinking she was asleep, two of the sisters discussed her in her presence. One mentioned that the child would go quickly to heaven, as she had never committed a sin. The child startled them by sitting up and remarking sadly and humbly, "Oh no, Mother, I told a lie once!"

On first seeing a statue of the Infant of Prague, Nellie questioned the nurse about it. Having been told the story of Christ as a child, Nellie often afterwards asked for the "story of Holy God when He was a little child." Someone suggested she join in a novena to the holy infant for her own health. She did, and at its conclusion there was a slight improvement and she was allowed to get up for several hours each day. Shortly afterwards when Nurse Hall suffered a minor illness, Nellie called one of the older girls and told her to "go and get Holy God and put him on the chair [near her bed]. I want to ask Him to make Mother better. He made me better, you know."

When possible, Nurse tried to carry Nellie out to the garden daily for the beneficial sunshine. They usually stopped at the convent chapel for a visit. Nellie came to understand the chapel as the "house of Holy God" where people went to "talk to Him." Sometimes Nurse would carry Nellie in her arms while she made the Stations of the Cross. At the picture of the crucifixion, Nellie asked why Holy God had allowed Himself to be hurt. Nurse then explained the passion in simple terms and at the conclusion Nellie burst into tears, sobbing "Poor Holy God! Poor Holy God!"

Even at this tender age, Nellie seemed to be able to grasp the concept of God present in the Blessed Sacrament. She seemed to have an intuition on days that Exposition or Benediction were to be held and asked to be taken to the chapel to see Holy God since he wasn't in "lockup." The true daughter of a soldier, she often used military terms. In the military, a jail is called a "lockup," and to Nellie's childish way of thinking the host in the tabernacle was captured. Later, when she was confirmed, she joyously told the sisters that "Now I am Holy God's little soldier."

After a few months in the infirmary, Nurse Hall had Nellie's bed moved to her quarters. Here, the affectionate child would often stick her little hand through the rails to hold Nurse's hand as she fell asleep. A little altar to the Holy Child was placed by her bed, and she delighted in the fresh flowers placed there. One day, the girl who was sitting with Nellie while Nurse Hall visited her other patients left the room for a few moments. On returning, she found Nellie clutching one of the flowers and attempting to climb back into bed. The girl scolded Nellie for being naughty and stealing a flower and threatened to tell Nurse on her return. Nellie just clutched the flower to her breast but later when she was alone with Nurse Hall she said, "Mother, I am sorry I took the flower. But I was only talking to Holy God and He gave me the flower. He did, Mother!" Childish prattle? Perhaps, although later events indicate that Nellie did indeed enjoy the special favor of conversation with Our Lord.

A short time later, Nellie told Nurse Hall and Sister Immaculata that Holy God had told her that she was not good enough to go yet. She continued by telling them that Holy God had come to stand by her bed. When they asked what He was like, she crossed her hands on her breast to indicate his appearance. Thinking it was just childish imagination, they decided not to say anything unless Nellie brought it up again.

By the end of September, Nellie's health was much worse. She complained of a sore throat, but after an examination by the doctor which found nothing wrong with her throat, Nurse discovered that a tooth had come in and become embedded in the root of her tongue, which must have been quite painful. Later, it was discovered that caries had attacked the bone of her jaw and eaten it partially away. At times, the bad odor from the diseased jaw was unbearable. Surprisingly, however, after Nellie made her First Communion the odor disappeared and was not noticed again.

For such a young child, Nellie had learned much of her religion. She had memorized the morning and evening prayers, the acts of faith, hope and charity, the principal mysteries and much of the story of the life of Jesus. When the sisters suggested that she unite her sufferings with those of Our Lord, she seemed to understand immediately. She kept a little crucifix by her bed, and when the pain was severe, she clutched it in her tiny hands and whispered, "Poor Holy God, poor Holy God," in a sort of chanted prayer. She prayed the Rosary, piously kissing each bead in a practice taught to her by her dead mother. Her spirit of recollection in daily prayer was remarkable for one so young.

Nellie was confirmed October 8, 1907, by the Most Rev. Dr. T. A. O'Callaghan, O.P. Although the sisters had offered prayers for the intention of Nellie's being confirmed before her death, they hadn't specifically brought the matter to the bishop, although they had written to him about the Organ girls. They were startled and joyous when he called to say he was coming to confirm Nellie. The sisters believed that this was a special inspiration, and many of the most extraordinary graces the child received were granted after her reception of this sacrament. The Bishop was visibly impressed by the piety of the little girl, and after the ceremony he met her in the parlor and gave her another blessing.

Nellie's soul began to be filled to overflowing with love for Jesus in the Real Presence, and she developed an insatiable desire to be united to God in Holy Communion. The sisters became aware of this through the child's remarks which, although expressed in childish language, indicated the yearning of a mature soul. Several times she was overheard whispering to herself in a sad tone, "I want Holy God! Oh! I wonder when He will come. I want Him to come into my heart." Nurse Hall, whose practice was to go to daily Mass before beginning her work, hesitated, seeing how weak Nellie had become and thinking it unsafe to leave her alone. But Nellie insisted, "Mother, go down to Holy Mass and get Holy God and come back to kiss me." After the kiss, Nellie indicated that Nurse should go back and make her thanksgiving; she herself didn't speak and seemed recollected in prayer. In her childish way, it seemed Nellie was sharing in Communion through the kiss.

One evening when Reverend Mother was visiting, Nellie asked her, "Mother, tomorrow morning when you get Holy God will you bring Him up to me?" Not knowing how to respond, the sister replied, "I will ask Holy God to be very fond of you, and I will come up to see you after Mass." The child seemed satisfied with that response, and the sister left. Later, Nellie told Nurse Hall, "Mother Francis is going to bring me Holy God in the morning."

Nellie was up before daybreak and woke Nurse Hall, insisting she get up and tidy the room to make ready for Holy God. Nellie waited anxiously, and when she saw Mother Francis enter without Holy God she broke into bitter weeping. Although she didn't ask again, Nellie fell into a protracted state of recollection for several days. Nurse Hall and Mother Francis feared the end was coming soon.

The sisters spoke with a Jesuit who was giving the annual community retreat, and he examined Nellie several times to discern if she had reached the age of reason and if she was, indeed, longing for the Sacrament. Pope Pius X had not yet issued his decree on the early Communion of young children, so for Nellie to be allowed to communicate would be a great exception to the ordinary practice. The Jesuit, Father Bury, finally wrote, "With regard to the reception of the Sacrament, Nellie had arrived at the use of reason. I firmly believe that the child was endowed in no ordinary degree with an ardent love of God, with an intense desire to be united to Him in Holy Communion." His conclusion was communicated to the Bishop, who gave his consent. On being told the news, Nellie joyfully exclaimed, "I will have Holy God in my heart!"

December 6, 1907, Nellie was dressed in a wreathed veil and a white gown and was carried down to receive, at last, Holy God in her heart. The same priest who had examined her wrote, "The child literally hungered for her God, and received Him from my hands in a transport of love." The children of the school burst into the joyous strains of the First Communion hymn as the tiny communicant sat motionless in loving conference with the Savior.

The following Sunday, Nellie was able to communicate again and was enrolled in the sodality of the Children of Mary. Proudly she received the ribbon and medal of the sodality with great devotion.

Nellie's condition deteriorated rapidly, and she was given extreme unction. Still, the little martyr lingered. When possible, she begged to be taken to the chapel to receive Holy God. Some days she whispered sadly, "Mother, I am too tired to go down to Holy God today," and her God was brought to her sickbed. Her recollected thanksgivings were remarkable for one so young. She seemed already to be living in the constant presence of God.

One morning, one of the sisters asked her, "Baby, when you go to Holy God tell him Mother Francis wants some money to pay her debts." With sublime confidence, Nellie told her confidently. "Holy God knows it and that's enough."

By January, it seemed almost miraculous that the child still lived. She could take and keep down only the tiniest portions of food. Her silent communion with God became longer and more frequent, and she often asked her caregivers to leave the room so she could speak with Holy God. When they asked her if she weren't lonely or afraid while they were out of the room, she replied, "Oh no! I was talking to Holy God." If they questioned her about the conversation she told them Holy God had told her not to talk about it.

One day, Reverend Mother showed Nellie a picture of the Sacred Heart and Nellie said, "That's not the way I saw Holy God." When asked what she meant, Nellie crossed her arms on her breast and told Reverend Mother how Holy God had stood by her bed. Reverend Mother then questioned Sister Immaculata and Nurse, who verified that Nellie had mentioned the incident to them.

True to her own prediction, Nellie's soul flew to Holy God on His own day, Sunday, February 2, 1908. They dressed her in her First Communion dress with its white wreath and veil. She was buried the following day in the public cemetery.

A year later, after receiving the necessary permission, Nellie's grave was opened in preparation to transfer her relics to the convent cemetery at Sunday's Well. The body was found intact with the exception of a small cavity in the right jaw. Her clothes were still intact and the medal of the sodality around her neck looked as if it had just been polished. ✢

10

Fathi Abboud Baladi

Lebanon, 1961–1980

A Star from the East

"Do you want to understand life? Hold a weeping infant in your arms. Dry the tears of a mother who has lost her child. Life is often hidden, but never completely disappears. Indeed, one can never forget past moments, nor the hours of childhood. One cannot forget those who have left us. Although they seem far from us, they are closer than ever; in silence, we hear their gentle voices; in their stillness, we see them in the act of moving. If you sometimes feel cold at night, look around you and notice those who are shivering even more than you, and you will be warmed. If you suffer hunger or thirst one day, look around you at those who are dying of hunger and thirst, and you will be calmed. Do not look for life in distant wonders, it is close to you in the very act of looking, it awaits you with arms outstretched, smiling, bearing the sheaf of wheat and heather of flower." So wrote the young Fathi Baladi in his spiritual journal.

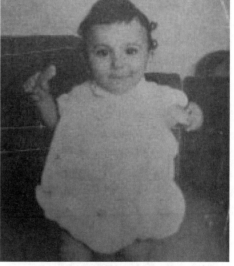
Fathi at one year old

Fathi Baladi, the only son of a pious Christian family belonging to the Melkite-Greek Catholic Church, was born September 22, 1961, in Beirut, Lebanon. Abboud Baladi, a bank manager, and his wife, Nelly Medawar-Baladi, lived their Christianity with conviction, and

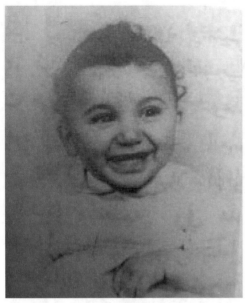

As a young child, Fathi had a sweet, calm temperament

passed this trait on to their three children, Nicole, Fathi, and Gina.

From the time he was a small child, Fathi saw life on earth as a gift given by God with a mandate for service to others. As a teenager, he wrote in his spiritual diary: "I believe in one God, whom I love: the one and only great God, in whom one must believe; ... for those whose life is no more a joy I pray; to those who suffer, starve or die, I cry for them. Children of the world, I love you. O my God, I love You! I swear You are great ... I thank You, O God, for having created me, for having adorned me, and for having glorified me."

Fathi's childhood was characterized by his eagerness to learn. He enjoyed school and he loved to read. Catechism and art were his favorite subjects. From the age of six, he particularly loved to draw pictures of the Virgin.

Fathi had a sweet, calm temperament, and was always obedient to his parents. Just like any other normal children, Fathi and his sisters shared their things and played together. Fathi, however, rarely engaged in the normal childhood scuffles or arguments. He was a tranquil child, and his sense of humor matched his tranquility. When the children were talking, Fathi would often say things that made his sisters laugh.

The rare times the Baladi children squabbled, little Gina was usually the instigator. Although she was also a good student, Gina loved to play, and when her brother tried to ignore her, she took his things and hid them. Even then, without becoming angry, he would try in a nice way to get her to leave him alone. Sometimes he resorted to making a deal with her to keep her from pestering him. One time he gave her some money, telling her that if she went to buy him some chocolate bars he would give her one of them plus a dollar.

Nicole was five years older than Fathi. The two used to talk about many things together. Once, Nicole tried to convince Fathi of some point which was not correct. After trying in vain to argue his side of the issue, Fathi took up his pencil and drew his response for her. When Nicole realized her mistake, the two smiled and hugged each other to end the argument.

Compassionate and helpful, Fathi often visited the elderly and the sick with his father. He enjoyed just talking and listening to them, kindly and respectfully.

Although Fathi never had a pet, he loved birds and often drew eagles on the covers of his notebooks. He could not bear to see a bird in a cage, however. Once when the family was staying at their home in the mountains, Mr. Baladi was helping his wife fix a window in the bedroom. He felt something brush his arm and captured a little bird that had flown in through the open window. Gina put the bird into a box which she put in a corner in the bathroom, intending to keep it for a pet. As young children will do, she then wandered off. Quietly, Fathi went in and, opening the bathroom window, allowed the bird to fly free.

Fathi at five

A bright student, he was always willing to help his classmates with their homework. He was so willing, in fact, that when a friend didn't really care about his schoolwork, Fathi offered to stay with him in the classroom during recess to help him do the assigned work.

When the school asked the children to bring donations for the poor, Fathi asked his mother to let him take some of his good clothes, not just the old, worn-out ones. He also asked for some of her homemade jam because it was so tasty he knew the poor would enjoy it. And, of course, he also would often give away his own pocket money.

Fathi began pre-school at Holy Wisdom School in Beirut, which he attended for two years. Then, at the age of five, he entered Sagesse school (Ashrafieh) until he began college classes. Here, when he was about ten years old, his spiritual director told him, "Fathi, one day you will be a great saint!" Today, that priest says that in the soul of Fathi he discovered an exceptional purity, an original innocence, and a soul attached to his Creator.

Fathi's spiritual director at Sagesse school told him, "Fathi, one day you will be a great saint!"

Apparently, Fathi had begun to think of a vocation to the priesthood. Twice he told his mother, "If I devote myself to the clerical life, I can accomplish great things."

At the age of eighteen, Fathi began his university studies in architecture at the Académie Libanaise des Beaux Arts (ALBA). This is the school of fine arts of the University of Saint John of Damascus (Balamand University). The young student had a passionate love for classical music, sculpture, painting, and the history of art and architecture. He was particularly enthralled by the beauty of the ancient cathedrals and of icons.

Lebanon has been torn with civil war for many years. Fathi, like many of the Lebanese youth, knew of the problems and prayed for their end. He shared the common human discouragement, but he took the problems of his country to God in prayer. Although he prayed for himself, his constant prayers were for others:

"I think that the future is dark, for I feel that the whole world is even more dark. I fear that the war will destroy both our hearts and our homes. One is sad for those who are loved. One must refuse to accept their death, their suffering, their exhaustion. One rebels; one is distraught; one grieves. Lord, hear this melody which is being sung;

do not leave us like this, O You who are so great and powerful. Look upon us! Remain in us.

"One is saddened, yes, for it is necessary. One weeps, for it is necessary to weep. One is left desolate in order to be found. And you decline all this; nevertheless, it is joyful. The tears are beautiful; sadness is a path to You; and solitude is a hymn of glory to Your greatness and to man.

Fathi, twelve years old

"Lord, do not abandon me. Do not abandon those who suffer, those who are hungry, thirsty, those who are bound by the cruelty of men, those who are behind the bars of prison. Do not forget those who are loved, who are lamented, who see life as of simple men, whom You love above all, and whom You look upon, lifting up the head as they smile and glorify Your goodness and strength. Lord, help us."

On New Year's Eve, 1980, Fathi was on his way to Araya to visit a fellow student, to wish him a Happy New Year and to review some of their classes in architecture. He did not return. His parents found him riddled with bullets, lying on the seat of his car. His arms were folded in the form of a cross. His face was serene, suggesting a peace of soul and resignation to his tragic fate.

Fathi was always a bright student

After Fathi's death, his mother looked through his notes and his books. She found an array of religious drawings and a number of prayers that he had written for the weak, the hungry, the miserable and prisoners. Fathi kept a spiritual journal, recording his thoughts, while the war in Lebanon evolved around him. His notes show a spiritual maturity rare in one so young.

Some days after the death of their son, his parents were favored with an amazing consolation. Plunged in grief, they suddenly heard the voice of their son, Fathi. He spoke with them, calling them by name. He told them not to grieve, assuring them that he was in heaven with the angels and saints. The house was suddenly permeated by the fragrance of exquisite incense and filled with a radiant light.

Fathi Abboud Baladi at age seventeen

Fathi was buried at the Greek Catholic cemetery of Beirut, which is located on the green line that once divided Beirut into two sectors.

Word of the consoling event experienced by Fathi's parents soon spread. Friends of the family, and then others, began to ask his intercession. Miraculous healings and apparitions began to be claimed. Soon these events were brought to the attention of the ecclesiastical authorities.

Fathi's body was transported to the monastery of Saint Saviour in Sarba, Jounieh, a house of the Aleppian Basilian Fathers. Many remarkable phenomena described as prodigies are attributed to his intercession, including cures, apparitions, lights, tongues of fire, voices, strains of music and fragrances of incense. To those, volumes of signed statements bear witness.

On July 30, 1994, the Holy Synod of the Melkite Church made the decision to begin the process of beatification and Fathi's cause was opened. It is still in the preliminary stages of the process. ✛

11

Faustino Pérez-Manglano
Spain, 1946–1963

A Boy Who Stormed the Goal

If we were to think of life as a soccer game, with heaven as the goal, then a seventeen-year-old Spanish boy, Faustino Pérez-Manglano, would be a World Cup forward. With his dream of a religious vocation and the love of the Virgin Mary as his "assists," Faustino stormed the goal with a "banana kick" around pain and illness and, with breakaway speed, headed home to win the match.

———

Faustino Pérez-Manglano Magro was born Sunday, August 4, 1946, in Valencia, Spain. He was the oldest of the four children of Faustino Pérez-Manglano Vidal, a gynecologist, and Maria de la Encarnacion Magro Alonso. They chose a unique birth announcement: a calendar page for the day. It marked the joyous point in time of the birth of their firstborn; perhaps it also symbolized the transitory nature of life itself. Faustino was baptized that same August and confirmed at the age of eight. Only a few calendars marked the years of Faustino's life on earth. Much like the sport he grew to love so well, he used these brief years in a rapid ascent to holiness.

Faustino began school at the age of four, a happy and curious child. The Loreto School was run by the Sisters of the Holy Family. One day, he took hold of one of the sisters' crucifixes and asked her who it was. She explained that it was Our Lord, and told how he was crucified. With all the simplicity of his young age, Faustino began to try and remove the nails, asking the sister, "But didn't you cry a lot when they nailed him?"

At six, Faustino enrolled at Our Lady of the Pillar School, run by the Marianists. From the beginning, he liked school. He got good grades and enjoyed the games and excursions. He loved nature, hiking, swimming, and camping.

During the school year, Faustino lived in Valencia, but he spent most summers, along with more than a dozen cousins, in Alicante, at the home of his grandparents. He made his First Communion in Alicante on July 4, 1954, together with his sister Maria Encarna and three cousins.

On his grandparents' farm, there was an orchard and a number of unused buildings that formed a natural playground for the lively children. They played soccer, hunted treasure, camped, and played make-believe as happy children normally do. At first, the oldest cousin, Augusto, was the natural leader; when he became too grown up for childish games, Faustino took his place. He seemed to get along well with the others — creating union — and his joyful smile and desire that everyone else feel happy brought a special peace.

Throughout his school years, Faustino was known as a good boy. One of his teachers commented that he was enthusiastic, joyful, and pious. But God seemed to demand more.

In October of 1959, at the age of thirteen, Faustino made his first retreat at Casa de la Purisima de Alacuas. He talked over a little problem with his spiritual director, Father José Maria Salaverri. He

Faustino - Relaxing at Járea with his parents

explained that he had made a promise to the Virgin when he was in fifth grade to pray the Rosary every day until 1961. Sometimes in the summers he had been distracted and failed to keep his promise but had kept track and was trying to catch up. Then he mentioned a number of Rosaries owed. The priest was shocked at the fidelity of the young boy. Wisely, the confessor told him to consider his debt cancelled and without any promises or keeping track to try and pray the Rosary as often as possible.

For the rest of his life, Faustino continued to pray the Rosary often.

One classmate remembers seeing Faustino walking ahead of him on the way to school one day. He hurried to catch up, and then realized that Faustino was praying the Rosary. He says, "Without saying anything, and with simplicity and naturalness, (Faustino) gathered it into his hand and put it into his Rosary case — all of this with a smile. He wasn't the least disturbed."

In the summer of 1960, Faustino began to write a

At age sixteen in Alicante, 1961

diary which he faithfully wrote in every day for a year and later continued in a sporadic manner. The first entry was written on September 14, 1960, and shows the beginning of the symptoms of the Hodgkin's disease that would eventually claim his life.

14–IX–60. I got up with the familiar pain. It left me. I finished Mario Gaitan. A beautiful book. I helped Fausto a little with watering. At quarter to nine I prayed the Rosary.

The first year of Faustino's diary seems to be little more than a timetable in which he recorded a few facts of the day. The second part is shorter and contains more personal reflection, usually of a spiritual nature. He was neither a literary artist nor a sentimentalist. He considered himself a poor writer, and he jokingly referred to his style in a letter to his cousin Augusto: "I tell you a lot, but in telegram form. I would like to do it some other way, but it just doesn't come out. Just a dull boy." In spite of his difficulty in expressing himself, his diary and some of his letters present a clear picture of how God was slowly seeping into every part of the fabric of his life.

Faustino was an avid fan of the Valencia soccer team, and in his diary records his love of the sport and the outcome of many of the team's games. And the missions — another of his loves — are often mentioned in his diary. In the entry for 19–X–60 he mentions his praying of the Rosary, the soccer score, and an auction held at school for the missions. "I got a pack of Chesterfields for 115 *pesetas*, which I gave back so they could auction it off again because I promised the Virgin I wouldn't smoke a single cigarette until summer. We have 1,558 *pesetas* for the missions now."

Faustino became ill in November 1960, and in January of the following year he wrote, "I am still ill and I don't know when I will be able to go to school. . . . Even though it costs me a lot to pray, I pray the Rosary every day, except a few days that I missed."

Faustino's illness kept him in bed for most of the year. There was a great deal of pain, along with strong medicine, injections, and radiotherapy. In spite of this, he continued to study at home so as not to lose the year.

In October 1960, Faustino had become an aspirant to the Marian sodality. He wrote, "It is a difficult plan, but I know I can do it." During retreat, he expressed his resolve: "I am going to try an asceticism of 'yes' to everything good."

During the annual retreat that year, Faustino's entry for October 22 reads, "We talked about many things, but one made an impression on me. What vocation am I going to choose? Doctor? Chemist? Or will I perhaps be a priest? That is what has impressed me. Has the Lord chosen me? He will tell me. How good it is here in Alcuas! For the day and a little that is left of the retreat, I'm going to remain completely silent. Maybe God will speak to me."

Faustino on the tower of Notre Dame in Paris, 1962

Apparently, in some way, God did speak to the soul of this young boy. The following day he wrote, "Father and I will keep the secret of my vocation until we see if I really have it. I'm about to burst with the immense happiness I have. How marvelous Christ is!"

Over the next two and a half years, Faustino mentions his vocation from time to time in his diary. Each time he seems more certain, more happy, with this direction for his life. For Faustino, this desire for a religious vocation became an instrument that helped him move rapidly towards sanctity. Feeling the call to God's service spurred his generosity and helped him to detach himself more and more from the things of earth, and to discover the redemptive value of suffering freely accepted in union with Christ. Although humanly speaking, Faustino didn't fulfill the call to a religious vocation, in his innermost being he lived it to the full. In January of 1962, a diary entry notes, "Sanctity is very difficult. But I will try, and who knows if I might achieve it?"

From November of 1960 to May of 1961, Faustino carried the cross that the Lord had given him — the pain and debilitation of a fatal form of Hodgkin's disease. During these months he records his pain and low spirits in his diary, but he accepted these without complaint, and he attempted to make certain that others did not suffer because of him. During this time, too, his infantile affection for the Virgin Mary began to change into a mature understanding of her role. "Every day I love

At his confirmation in 1955

Mary more. She is my Mother. Thanks to her, each day I love my own mother more." Where previously his diary had been sparse in sentiments, he now begins to express himself in a fuller way. "Jesus, let me love Mary, not only because she is pure, beautiful, good, compassionate, my Mother, but because she is Your mother and You love her infinitely. . . . If I want to imitate Christ, my Master, I must do it by infinitely loving what He infinitely loves, His Mother and mine."

Faustino's health seemed to improve. With his family, he made trips to Zaragoza to visit the Lady of the Pillar, and to Lourdes. After months of suffering, he felt very well, although his physical appearance was not attractive. The chemotherapy had caused him to bloat and to lose his hair. When his mother asked if it didn't bother him for people to see him like that, he responded "Why? There's nothing bad about it. If your hair falls out, what are you going to do? It will grow back." Then he added, laughing, "What went away will come back again."

At Lourdes, Faustino tells us, "It's moving to be with all the sick and to see their resignation and faith. . . . Afterwards, I helped as a *brancardier* [stretcher bearer], helping at the pools and at the Grotto." And, again, "I think the greatest miracle of Lourdes is the conversions that take place there. It's phenomenal to see how very sick people don't ask for their own health, but for that of those at their side. . . . The next time I go to Lourdes I will go as a *brancardier*." As always, Faustino thought more of others than of himself.

In the summer of 1961, Faustino was told to "take it easy." With friends, he took walks through the country, fished, and practiced target shooting with a rifle. Swimming was forbidden, but he accepted both the good and the bad tranquilly. His grandmother remembered that since he wasn't very strong, with each meal they gave him a glass of milk with *Cola-cao*. That Christmas, when the cousins were discussing their likes and dislikes regarding beverages, Faustino, without thinking, said, "What I can't stand is *Cola-cao*. It makes me nauseous." Startled, his grandmother asked why he hadn't mentioned that the previous summer. Faustino replied, "Grandmother, you did it with so much pleasure that I didn't want to deprive you of the enjoyment." Time and again, Faustino subjugated his own wishes and preferences in favor of others.

That winter, Faustino begged to be allowed to go camping with his friends. His parents refused to allow it, saying that he could go in the spring if his health was still improving. He wrote in his diary, "I had a great disappointment. . . . Thanks be to God it has left me and

I will offer it up for the missions. . . . I will make the sacrifice and will suffer willingly for the missions."

On retreat in January 1962, he reflected on his vocation and began to learn detachment. "I think my vocation is out of love for Christ, with infinite desire to serve him in the best way possible. That desire includes, if it might be necessary, dying for Him." By nature a saver, Faustino did not like to spend his money on frivolous things. During this retreat, he surprised his spiritual director by saying he felt he was too attached to money. He took his savings and sent them, in the form of books, to the missions in Japan.

Faustino began to think about the problems of the world. He wrote, "For a great many Christians, God is a problem. They don't want God to bother or disturb them." The topic was discussed in greater depth in sodality meetings, and Faustino began to take a great interest in sociology classes. "We have life too easy. We are in danger. We have only comforts and not one difficulty worth mentioning. Everything as we want it. We have to be simple, . . ." Not content with theories, Faustino concentrated on the concrete, and did small things that were within his grasp. He and his friend Ernesto took an inter-

Faustino (second from right) in Verrano, 1956

est in a young working boy of fourteen. They helped him with clothes, food, and medicine as well as visiting with him as a friend.

During the spring of 1962, Faustino's parents at last allowed him

Faustino was always the leader

to go camping again. Wisely, they chose to let him enjoy a full life in the short time God had left to him. In spite of his physical limitations, he enjoyed it immensely. In June, he made his first promises in the sodality. In the summer came a final glorious camping trip with school companions to France and Switzerland. In one of his notes we read, "I tried to be as serviceable as possible." Indeed, his companions underline the fact that this was a part of his nature and that he was always ready to do a favor.

His pre-university year was his final year of school. By the fall, his sickness had obviously returned in full force. The medicine was not helping, and his mother had to help the determined student to dress and get him off to school. He could only remain a half day, and in the afternoons he studied in bed. By January of 1963, he was swollen, in pain, and albumin was forming. He made his final school act — the annual retreat — towards the end of the month. In his retreat notes there is a moving reflection on death: "We must accept death as of now. A death with the Virgin is marvelous. Christ, grant that every day I may be more devoted to Mary. I want to be always intimately united to her. She will help me to die, and I will have the death of a true saint. Let death come when God wants and where God wants. It will come at the time, the place, and in the way that is best for me, sent by Our Father, God. Welcome to our sister, death."

Several times during this retreat he wrote, "Most Holy Virgin, teach me to see the value of suffering. Teach me, Lord, the value of suffering."

On February 4, the priest decided to speak frankly with Faustino, and told him the seriousness of his illness. Faustino commented wryly, "I thought the doctors were at their wits' end."

"And are you ready to die if God wishes it?" his confessor asked.

"What do you think, Father: I'm prepared, right?"

Fighting to hold back tears, Faustino confessed, "It's only that I feel sorry for Papa and Mama. How sad they are going to be!"

On February 9, he received the sacrament of the sick. In his final diary entry, he expresses his happiness to have received extreme unction, "It's marvelous to have received it knowing completely what was received." He renewed his sodality promises and wrote "Help me to continue offering these little inconveniences for the needs of the world."

Going on retreat in 1959

A normal boy, Faustino enjoyed the visits of his classmates and their chatter about the daily occurrences at school. He read a lot, prayed, and received daily Communion. His spiritual director, Father Salaverri, visited and asked him if he kept in mind the goals he had made on retreat. "Yes Father, to become a saint."

"Good, but are you trying to do so?"

Smiling broadly, Faustino answered, "Here I am. I think this is a good method, right?"

Sunday, March 3, Father Salaverri visited and, in spite of Faustino's failure to complain, it was obvious that he was suffering. His hands were shaking, and when the priest asked him if he was nervous, Faustino replied, "No Father, it's the body. I haven't been able to sleep for so long. But inside, I'm at peace."

The priest gave him several requests for heaven, the first being to console his parents, and Faustino promised to carry them out. Then he gave the boy wonderful news. He promised to return the following day to receive Faustino's vows as a Marianist. Special permission had just been received based on his wish and the extreme seriousness of his condition. Instead, Faustino became a Marianist only by desire.

The painful hours dragged by and the edema began to fill his lungs. At eleven he asked for a drink and, noticing his mother there, he told her to go to bed and rest. A few minutes later he called her back to help him. As she held him, he gave a sudden jolt and then lay lifeless in his mother's arms.

Faustino Pérez-Manglano was a normal and happy boy who radiated joy and serenity. His reputation for sanctity led to the idea of the introduction of his cause for beatification. In 1986, his remains were transferred from the cemetery of Valencia to the chapel of Our Lady of the Pillar school. On this occasion, the Superior General of the Marianists said, "His silent presence will be an incentive for everyone: teachers, parents, students. He will remind us that in this life we must not be content with little, but that it is possible to — and we should do so — strive for a high human and Christian ideal to better the world." ✢

12

Blessed Francisco Marto
Portugal, 1908-1919

Blessed Jacinta Marto
Portugal, 1910–1920

Young Seers of Fátima

When Francisco and Jacinta Marto were beatified in 2001, they were the first children non-martyrs this young to ever be acclaimed with this honor. Many believed their beatification ratified the declaration of Vatican Council II that all Christians are called to holiness (Dogmatic Constitution on the Church, 40-42) by confirming that this even included children. The young brother and sister were not beatified because of their visions of the Virgin. Instead, they are held up as models of heroic virtue, practiced faithfully although in the manner appropriate to children.

———

On May 13, 1917, the Blessed Virgin Mary appeared to three young shepherd children in the village of Aljustrel in Fátima, Portugal. After promising to take them to heaven, she asked, "Are you willing to offer yourselves to God and bear all the sufferings He wills to send you, as an act of reparation for the sins by which He is offended and of supplication for the conversion of sinners?"

"Yes, we are willing," was their reply.

"Then you are going to have much to suffer, but the grace of God will be your comfort."

The three children agreed not to tell anyone about what they had seen. But that night, feeling unable to keep silent, seven-year-old Jacinta Marto told her mother the story of how she had seen a beautiful lady. Her nine-year-old brother, Francisco, confirmed his sister's story, as did their cousin, Lucia dos Santos, age ten. The account was received by their families, and later by ecclesiastical and civil authorities, with skepticism and disbelief. But the Church has subsequently

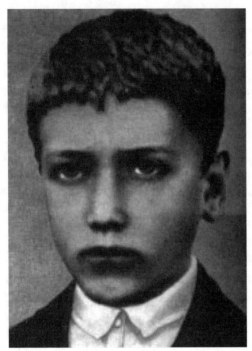

Blessed Francisco Marto

approved the apparitions of Fátima, declaring that they are of particular significance for our own times.

The vision had been preceded by several visits of an angel, who called himself the Angel of Peace, who had knelt and bowed his head to the ground, teaching the children prayers of reparation. On his second visit he told the children, "Offer prayers and sacrifices constantly to the Most High." On his third visit, the angel held a chalice; suspended above it was a Host. He made the children recite with him three times a prayer of reparation and of supplication for sinners. Then, giving the Host to Lucia and the Blood from the chalice to Francisco and Jacinta, he said, "Take and drink the Body and Blood of Jesus Christ, horribly outraged by ungrateful men! Repair their crimes and console your God." Then he prostrated himself and recited the prayer three more times. Not realizing that he had received Communion, Francisco later said, "I felt that God was in me, but I didn't know how it was."

On the day of the first apparition, the children had taken their flocks to the Cova da Iria, a rocky little knoll about a mile and a half from Fátima. There they tended the sheep and played games.

Suddenly, a great wind arose and they were frightened by a flash of light. A brilliant white light moved toward them, stopping at last on top of a small holm oak tree. Within the light they saw a lady, more brilliant than the sun; she told them that she was from heaven. She also told them to make sacrifices and to pray the Rosary every day for peace in the world, promising to return on the 13th of each month until the following October. At the apparitions of the angel and of Our

Lady, Francisco saw all the visions but did not hear them. Jacinta and Lucia both saw and heard them. Lucia alone spoke with Our Lady.

At each of the six apparitions, the Blessed Virgin Mary asked for the daily Rosary. She repeatedly asked for prayer and penances for the conversion of sinners and in reparation to her immaculate heart.

In June, a small crowd accompanied the three children to the Cova. The people could see only a small white cloud atop the holm oak tree, but the children's actions began to convince some people of the miraculous events taking place.

In July, about 5,000 people attended. At this time, Our Lady promised a great miracle for October 13. She said to the children, "Sacrifice yourselves for sinners, and say many times, especially whenever you make some sacrifice, "O Jesus, it is for love of Thee, for the conversion of sinners and in reparation for the sins committed against the immaculate heart of Mary."

The Blessed Mother then showed the children a terrifying vision of hell. She told them, "You have seen hell, where the souls of poor sinners go. To save them, God wishes to establish in the world devotion to my immaculate heart." She promised that if her requests were granted, many souls would be saved and there would be peace — but otherwise, "Russia will spread her errors throughout the world," and many sufferings and punishments would come upon the world. In fact, the Russian Revolution took place in October of that year.

The children suffered much from the skepticism of many people. In August, the anticlerical administrator of the district had the children arrested and placed in prison, and then he threatened to fry them in

Icon of Francisco Marto
by Rev. William Hart McNichols

oil if they persisted in their story. The children steadfastly refused to deny the visions. Finally they were released.

They had spent August 13 in jail, but on August 19 they saw the Blessed Mother. Looking very sad, she told them to "pray very much, and make sacrifices for sinners; for many souls go to hell because there are none to sacrifice themselves and pray for them."

On October 13, an estimated 70,000 people gathered at the Cova da Iria to see the promised miracle. A torrential rain fell all morning and the whole area was a sea of mud. At the appointed time, there was again a flash of light, and in a dazzling light, Our Lady appeared to the children. She requested that a chapel be built there to her honor, and she showed three scenes to the children: first, the Holy Family; second, Our Lord with the Mother of Sorrows beside Him; finally, Our Lady crowned as Queen of Heaven, holding the Divine Child on her knee and extending the Carmelite scapular to the crowd.

Suddenly, Lucia cried out, "Look at the sun!" The rain had abruptly stopped, and the sun seemed to spin about on its axis, then to descend toward the earth. Meanwhile, clouds, people, and other objects appeared to change colors constantly in the sun. As the sun

Blessed Jacinta Marto

appeared to descend, many fell to their knees in terror, begging pardon for their sins. Then, suddenly, the downward course of the sun stopped, and it resumed its normal position. Those present discovered that their clothes were completely dry. Thousands of eyewitnesses have testified to the miraculous events of that day.

By the end of October, 1918, scarcely a year later, both Francisco and Jacinta Marto had fallen ill, as predicted by Our Lady. Francisco died on April 4, 1919; Jacinta suffered a little longer until February 20, 1920, when she, too, went to God.

Francisco and Jacinta were the youngest of the eleven children of the Marto family. The family was poor, and the children had to help with earning a living. At the time of the apparitions, none of the children attended school or had learned to read.

Jacinta was endowed with a sweet and affectionate nature. She was also vivacious and somewhat capricious. Francisco on the other hand was quiet and submissive by nature. Jacinta loved dancing and playing games. She also wanted to win all of the games she played and would pout if she were the loser. Francisco preferred to play the flute while the others danced, and at games he never cared if he won.

The two children preferred to play with their cousin Lucia and were often present at the catechism lessons that Lucia's mother gave her children and the other children of the neighborhood for whom she babysat. Even from this early age, Jacinta had a great love for Our Lord. Once, when she had lost at a game of forfeits, Jacinta was told that her forfeit would be to give a hug and a kiss to one of her male cousins. She protested, "That, no, tell me to do some other things. Why don't you tell me to go and kiss Our Lord over there?" She pointed to a crucifix, "Very well," the winner said, "bring Him here and give Him three hugs and three kisses."

"To Our Lord, yes, I'll give as many as you like!" She ran and got the crucifix and kissed and embraced it with devotion. Then, looking attentively at the figure she asked, "Why is Our Lord nailed to a cross like that?" When she heard the answer, she cried, saying, "I'll never sin again! I don't want Our Lord to suffer any more."

Francisco had a naturally calm temperament and was extremely good-natured. Once, he brought a handkerchief with a picture of Our Lady on it to show to Lucia and the other children. He was very proud of it, for a friend had brought it to him from the seaside. It was passed from hand to hand, and in a few minutes it disappeared. The children looked for the handkerchief, and a little later Lucia found it in another small boy's pocket. This boy insisted that the handkerchief was his own, and that someone had brought him a handkerchief from the seaside also. To end the argument, Francisco said, "Let him have it. What does a handkerchief matter to me?"

Francisco liked animals. He once paid another boy two coins to free a bird he had caught. He would play with snakes and would pour milk into a hollow in the rock for them to drink. Francisco liked to be alone to pray and offer sacrifices; he would even go off apart from Lucia and Jacinta when the three were with the sheep. When Our Lady promised to take Francisco to heaven, she had added, "But he must say many Rosaries." When Lucia and Jacinta told him this, he exclaimed, "Oh, my dear Our Lady! I'll say as many Rosaries as you want!" From then on Francisco would often move off from the other two, and when they asked what he was doing he would hold up his Rosary. "Don't you remember that Our Lady said I must pray many Rosaries?"

When the children were wondering what they could offer as a sacrifice, Francisco suggested giving their lunch to the sheep; this was quickly done. Jacinta soon gave up the dancing she had so loved. Francisco said he no longer wanted to sing songs after seeing the angel and Our Lady. The little shepherds began to give their lunch to poor children every day, eating pine nuts and other things they could find in the pastures. They often made the sacrifice of doing without even a drink of water on those long hot days when they were parched with thirst.

As news of the apparitions spread, there were many visitors who came questioning the children; this was a great trial for them. They would often, when they saw such visitors approaching, take off and hide. Sometimes, however, there was no way to escape, and the children had to console themselves with offering up the sacrifice. Francisco once said, referring to Our Lord, "I offer Him all the sacrifices I can think of. Sometimes I don't even run away from all those people, just in order to make sacrifices!"

One day Lucia found a rope, and the children cut it into three pieces so that all three could tie a piece around their waists as a mortification. Sometimes this was so painful that Jacinta could not keep back her tears, but when Lucia urged her to remove it, she answered, "No! I want to offer this sacrifice to Our Lord in reparation, and for the conversion of sinners."

On September 13, Our Lady said to the three children, "God is pleased with your sacrifices, but He does not want you to sleep with the rope on; only wear it during the day."

Once, Lucia asked Francisco, "Which do you like better, to console Our Lord or to convert sinners so that their souls won't go to hell?" Francisco answered, "I'd rather console Our Lord ... I want first to console Our Lord and then convert the sinners so that they will not offend Him any more."

Francisco was also constantly occupied with thoughts of "the hidden Jesus" in the tabernacle. Sometimes he would spend hours on his knees in church. Francisco would encourage the other two children in making sacrifices.

Blessed Jacinta at the time of the apparitions

Francisco fell victim to the influenza epidemic which struck in autumn of 1918. After his first attack he recovered somewhat, but then relapsed in January. He suffered much, but still he always seemed joyful and contented. He often said to Lucia, "Look! Go to the church and give my love to the hidden Jesus. What hurts me most is that I cannot go there myself and stay awhile with the hidden Jesus."

By the first of April, Francisco was so weak that he could hardly speak. His greatest desire was to make his First Communion, and he asked that Lucia come to see him. When she came, he said, "I am going to confession. I am going to receive Holy Communion, and then I am going to die. I want you, Lucia, to tell me if you have ever seen me commit any sin. And I want Jacinta to tell me too."

Lucia recalled a few times Francisco had disobeyed his mother, running off to be with her or to hide when he had been told to stay home. Francisco said, "That's true." He sent Lucia to ask Jacinta the same question. Jacinta remembered a time when he and some other boys had thrown stones at each other; and once, a long time ago, he had stolen a *tostao* from his father to buy a hand organ.

"I've already confessed those sins, but I will confess them again. Perhaps it is for these sins of mine that Our Lord is so sad." Folding his hands he recited the prayer told to the children by Our Lady: "O my Jesus, forgive us our sins, save us from the fire of hell; lead all souls to heaven, especially those in most need of Thy mercy."

Francisco made his First Communion on the morning of April 3, 1919. He was radiant with joy, having received the hidden Jesus into his heart. He died the next day.

Both Lucia and Jacinta missed Francisco terribly. Lucia said, "This grief was a thorn that pierced my heart for years to come." Jacinta would spend time lost in thought about Francisco, and her eyes would fill with tears when she spoke of him.

Jacinta's life was marked by constant concern over the "poor sinners" in danger of hell. She often sat on the ground and thought about this, exclaiming out loud, "Oh, hell! Hell! How sorry I am for the souls who go to hell. And the people down there, alive, like wood in the fire!" Shuddering, she would recite the prayer taught by Our Lady: "O my Jesus, forgive us our sins, . . ." Lucia said of Jacinta that "every penance and mortification was as nothing in her eyes if it could only prevent souls from going to hell." Jacinta urged Francisco to pray for souls, exclaiming, "So many go there! So many!" She would say, "Why doesn't Our Lady show hell to sinners? If they saw it, they would not sin, so as to avoid going there! . . . I'm so sorry for sinners! If only I could show them hell!" Lucia told her not to be afraid, since she was going to heaven, but Jacinta answered, "I want all those people to go there too."

Jacinta fell ill with influenza shortly before Francisco took the disease. Our Lady had let her know that she would be sent to two hospitals and that she would die all alone in the second one. This prospect filled her with great sorrow and fear. She clung to Lucia and sobbed, "I'll never see you again! Nor my mother, nor my brothers, nor my father! I'll never see anyone ever again! And then I'll die all alone!" Jacinta then said, "O Jesus! Now You can convert many sinners, because this really is a big sacrifice!"

Many people came to see Jacinta in her sickroom at home because they sensed something supernatural in her presence. Women would bring their sewing to her bedside and sit by the holy child. If anyone spoke of someone and a particular sin, she would say, "Tell them not to do that, for it is a sin. They offend the Lord our God, and later they could be damned."

Before leaving for the hospital, Jacinta would force down the milk and broth her mother wanted her to take, declining the grapes she would have preferred. She would also give up a drink of water even when she was very thirsty. No sacrifice was too great for her beloved sinners.

Jacinta once said to Lucia, "I so like to tell Jesus that I love Him! Many times, when I say it to Him, I seem to have a fire in my heart, but it doesn't burn me." She also said, "I so love the immaculate heart of Mary! It is the heart of our dear Mother in heaven! Don't you love saying many times over, 'Sweet heart of Mary, immaculate heart of Mary'? I love it so much, so very much."

One day Lucia gave Jacinta quite a nice holy card picture of Jesus. Jacinta thought it was "so ugly" in contrast to Our Lord, who was so beautiful. But she wanted it anyway; she said, "It is He just the same."

Jacinta told Lucia that she was suffering a lot but that she was offering everything for sinners and in reparation to the immaculate heart of Mary. "Oh, how much I love to suffer for love of them (Jesus and Mary), just to give them pleasure! They greatly love those who suffer for the conversion of sinners!"

Jacinta had an open wound and a drain in her chest; it had to be dressed daily. Painful as this was, Lucia says that she bore it "without complaint and without the least sign of irritation." A priest described how Jacinta looked: "A living skeleton, her arms nothing but bones, her face all eyes, her cheeks wasted away by fever."

As Our Lady had foretold, Jacinta was sent to two hospitals. At the second one, in Lisbon, she underwent an operation in which two of her ribs were removed. The surgery had to be performed with only local anesthesia, since Jacinta was so weak. During the ordeal she repeated Our Lady's name over and over.

In Lisbon, Jacinta had stayed for a time in an orphanage run by Mother Godinho. This sister recorded some of the sayings of little Jacinta during those days. They included the following: "More souls go to hell because of sins of the flesh than for any other reason. Many marriages are not good; they do not please Our Lord and are not of God! People are lost because they do not think of the death of Our

Lord and do not do penance. If men only knew what eternity is, they would do everything in their power to change their lives."

On February 20, in the hospital, Jacinta called the nurse and asked for the last sacraments, saying she was about to die. The priest heard her confession and promised to bring her Holy Communion in the morning. Jacinta pleaded with him not to delay, telling him she would die that very night, but he did not feel that her end was so near. Jacinta did die that night, all alone, as Our Lady had foretold.

Sometime earlier, Jacinta had summed up Lucia's mission in these words: "It will not be long now before I go to heaven. You will remain here to make known that God wishes to establish in the world devotion to the immaculate heart of Mary. . . . Tell everybody that God grants us graces through the immaculate heart of Mary, that people are to ask her for them and that the heart of Jesus wants the immaculate heart of Mary to be venerated at His side. Tell them also

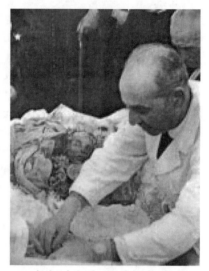

Jacinta's body was found to be incorrupt at the ritual exhumation before her beatification

to pray to the immaculate heart of Mary for peace, since God has entrusted it to her."

After Jacinta's death, Lucia was sent away to a boarding school by the bishop. Later, she became a Sister of Saint Dorothy. Twenty-nine years after the apparitions, she was permitted to revisit Fátima before becoming cloistered as a Carmelite nun. She lives today in the cloister at Coimbra, Portugal.

It is to Lucia that we are indebted for much of our information on Francisco and Jacinta. Her memoirs contain much information about them, and are a precious document of the workings of grace in these two souls. ✚

13

Venerable Galileo Nicolini
Italy, 1882–1897

Nothing Is Small

"Nothing is small that has reference to God. This defect in itself is a little defect but it offends the Infinite God. Therefore it is big. This act of virtue is in itself small, but it honors the Infinite God; therefore it is great." So wrote a young Passionist student, Galileo Nicolini, who at an early age learned the value of small things done for God. A contemporary of Saint Thérèse of Lisieux, he never knew of her or read about her "little way," yet his life is an example of one who followed that way and who knew the value of even the smallest things done for God.

———

Galileo Nicolini was born at Capranica, a small town near Rome, on June 17, 1882. Following the custom of the time, he was baptized four days later. He was confirmed at the age of six.

His father owned a construction business and was hard-working and hard-headed. Galileo inherited his father's spirit of determination and in time used it on his walk to holiness.

Galileo's cousin, Amabile, encouraged him in the Faith and counseled him to keep a small book of spiritual sayings, which he did. This first book developed into a collection, as he continued the practice for the rest of his short life. Far from being merely a book of sayings, though, these "spiritual diaries" became guidebooks to help Galileo on his ascent to sanctity.

A diligent and precocious student, Galileo did well in school. He began school at the age of three, and by the age of seven he could read and write so well that he handled his father's business correspondence. In short, Galileo was what today we might term a "bookworm." His mother testified that he was "crazy for study" and when she looked for him during the day he was most often in some secluded nook with his favorite books.

Galileo had religious teachers until the age of seven. Then he was required to attend a public school in order to take the entrance exam for high school. Although the friars taught all the subjects required by the civil authorities, the anti-clerical government did not recognize their schools.

Galileo (on the right) at the age of six, with his little brother Corrado.

Because he was so far advanced in his studies, and because of his religious convictions, once some schoolmates began to harass him. They gave him nicknames: "big eyes," "dude," and "proud." They followed him with catcalls, chucked stones at him and chalked offensive remarks on the town walls. At first, the eight-year-old bore these trials with great patience and silence, determined to imitate the suffering Savior. Eventually, however, his anger got the best of him, and one day, much to their surprise, his classmates discovered he was every bit as good with his fists as with his Rosary and books. After this, they ceased to bother him.

Eventually, his peers grew to like him very much. Galileo became an ardent apostle among the other students, as well as a lively participant in their games.

Once, a rather pompous businessman was a dinner guest at the Nicolini home. He made the remark that the friars taught nothing but nonsense at their inferior school. Nine-year-old Galileo immediately piped up, "Is that right, sir? You'd have to prove that to me. I've been at that school for some years now and I have yet to hear anything you describe. Would you be so kind as to make a list of these for me?" Having had his bluff called, the anti-clerical man tried to bully and berate religion in general. Galileo refuted each statement to the satisfaction and even approval of some other anti-clericals who were present. Later that evening the boy confided to his mother, "When that man was going against the Church today, I felt like a lion and could have torn him apart!"

Galileo burned with the desire to make his First Communion. He pestered his parish priest for all the information possible on the Blessed Sacrament, and made a special study of the young saints Stanislaus and Aloysius at the time of their First Communion. Then he went with the Passionist Fathers to Ritiro Sant' Angelo for a ten-day retreat. Here, at last, at the age of twelve, Galileo was allowed to receive the Sacrament for the first time on August 26, 1894. For Galileo, this was more than just First Communion; it was a turning point in his life.

Back home, Galileo told his confessor that he felt that Christ was calling him to be a Passionist. Father Callistus, who had prepared him for his Communion, was impressed with the child's unusual piety and asked him, "Tell me, Galileo, did Jesus say nothing in your heart?" Although he told Father that indeed he had received a communication, at first he only told him he would discuss it later. A few days later he confessed, "Jesus in my First Communion with Him made me see that I should become a Passionist . . . I feel that he wants great things from me."

Earlier, Galileo had expressed a desire to become a missionary, but from the time of his First Communion, he felt the clear call to the Passionist life. His family testified that he became very fervent, attending daily Mass and studying the practice of prayer. He presented himself personally at the Passionist Retreat of Saint Angelo and requested admission.

On learning that he was only twelve years old, the Passionist superior felt that he was too young to enter the community and refused to even consider it. His parents also flatly refused to think of allowing him to do so. His father, in particular, was against the idea. Because of his precocious intelligence, Galileo had become a valued worker in his father's business even at this early age, and his father was loathe to lose him. In addition, he was the oldest and favorite son. A Passionist friend pointed out the austerity of the Passionist life and advised him to wait. A wealthy uncle attempted to bribe him to forget the idea. Galileo merely answered, "This is my resolve and no one will move me from it."

Galileo's determination never faltered. Week after week he rode his donkey to the retreat to beg admittance. Week after week, the answer was "no."

About this time, Galileo's beloved cousin Amabile died of tuberculosis. Before her death, Galileo had helped care for the invalid. One of the Passionists suggested that Galileo make a novena, asking the aid of Our Lady of Pompei and of Amabile. At the end of the novena, his parents gave in and consented to his strong desire, and the

Passionists allowed him to enroll in their high school seminary in Rocca di Papa. His father not only consented, but came to the monastery with him to make the final arrangements himself.

Galileo loved the minor seminary where he cheerfully grew in holiness under the strict regime. He got along well with his companions and joined a confraternity dedicated to Our Lady of the Sacred Heart. He kept a calendar with Our Lady's feasts marked with reminders for special devotions for

School portrait of Galileo at the age of nine, made in the school year 1890-1891

their celebration. On it, he wrote, "No grace comes from God which does not pass through the hands of Our Lady. If, therefore, I wish to obtain all the graces necessary for perseverance to the end in the way I have chosen, I must have a tender and filial devotion to the Mother of God." Because of his excellent progress, Galileo was given a special dispensation and allowed to enter the novitiate at Lucca in 1896 at the age of fourteen. After the customary spiritual exercises, he was invested with the black habit of the Passionists and received his religious name: Confrater Gabriel of Our Lady of the Sacred Heart.

Galileo continued writing in his spiritual notebooks. In addition to his examination of his progress and his notes on the lives of the saints, his insight into the love of the Sacred Heart is outstanding for a fourteen-year-old. His notes on the Passion and the Blessed Sacrament as they relate to the Sacred Heart of Jesus seem to indicate that he had received extraordinary graces.

Much of the advice Galileo wrote in his notebook for himself is helpful to anyone wanting to draw closer to God. For example, he wrote: "In prayer be quiet, tranquil, with the knowledge of your own nothingness. . . . Do not be disturbed if the Lord does not show his face. . . . Use this opportunity to remain humble. Seek the cause; if it comes from yourself, remove it; if it is a trial from God, humbly bow your head. . . ."

After a few months in the novitiate, Galileo realized that he had tuberculosis. He knew the symptoms from having nursed his cousin; he knew also that the disease was fatal. He said nothing for fear of being sent home. After a year of silent suffering, he had a severe hemorrhage and finally told his superiors. Instead of sending him home, they transferred him to Monte Argentario, hoping that a change of air would help him.

Galileo arrived at the mountain monastery at the beginning of May 1897, and was immediately put to bed. One of the fathers wrote to the shrine of Our Lady of Pompeii, asking Bartolo Longo and his orphans to pray for Galileo's recovery. At the end of the letter, Galileo wrote a note to the Virgin: "Dear Mama, I am very sick. No one but you can cure me. Restore me to health if it be for the glory of God and the good of my soul."

About a week before his death, his mother came to visit. The monks were cloistered with papal enclosure, so she could not enter. After a hurried consultation with the superior, the novice master found the solution: the invalid's cot was taken outside the cloister so they could talk. How her heart must have ached to see her helpless son whose emaciated hands lay on the coverlet. His cheeks were flushed with fever and his large eyes were unnaturally bright. As she embraced him, he smiled to reassure her. After an all-too-brief visit, as she bent to kiss him goodbye, she asked her son if he was happy in such a strict order. He replied, "I have never regretted a minute of it!" When she pointed out that he was dying young, he replied, "But, Mama, if God wants to take me home now I am perfectly content. I am only sorry I couldn't have lived long enough to attain the perfection I intended as a good Passionist."

On his sick bed, Galileo prayed constantly. Since lengthy concentration is fatiguing to the sick, he occupied his time with vocal prayer. He kept a number of chaplets by his bed and prayed them one after the other; first the Rosary, then the Chaplet of the Seven Dolours, then the Five Wound beads, and then others.

He remained cheerful and his spiritual director wrote, "What I admired most in him was his remarkable patience. Never a complaint; never the slightest token of displeasure with the will of God. ... In moments of his greatest agony I hear him repeat 'Lord, increase my sufferings but increase also Thy grace.'" His one worry was that he was a burden to the community, and as he thanked the infirmarians for their help, he also begged their pardon for causing them any inconvenience.

At last, he was told that he was in imminent danger and asked if he would receive extreme unction. Galileo received the sacrament of the sick fervently, then smiled and murmured, "Oh my father, how beautiful to die like this." On the morning of May 13, he asked the infirmarian to light all the candles around the image of Our Lady of Pompeii and to call the religious to gather around him. When the other Passionists arrived, Galileo sat up in bed and repeated the Ave

Drawing of Galileo in his novice's habit

Maria several times. Then, pointing toward the picture of Our Lady, he suddenly exclaimed, "The saints!" and motioned for the brethren to make way. He sat up as if to greet visitors, then all trace of pain disappeared from his face and his color returned to normal as he sank back upon his pillow with his eyes closed.

As was the custom, his body was placed in a coffin and prepared for burial. The following morning, after Mass for the repose of his soul, the coffin was carried by the religious in procession to the neighboring town of Porto Santo Stefano for burial. In some way, the news had spread that a saint had died in the monastery, and outside the town a large number of people met the funeral cortege. They insisted on seeing the "little saint," so the casket was opened in the roadway.

Another crowd had gathered in the parish church and the casket had to be opened again. The people pressed around, touching the body with their Rosaries. Some began to snip away pieces of the tunic and strands of hair. At last, to satisfy the devotion of the people, a large piece of the habit was cut off and cut into small pieces and distributed to those present.

At the cemetery, people kept thronging. So the body was left exposed for two days with candles kept burning around it and fresh flowers heaped on it in profusion. Finally, on the third day, the burial

Last photo of Galileo in his Passionist habit, taken on the day of his death

was completed. Galileo's earthly remains rested in the cemetery of Porto Santo Stefano for two years.

Devotion to the saintly young Passionist began to spread throughout the world, and demands for a beatification process to be opened at last caused the Passionists to call for a canonical recognition of the relics. At the exhumation, the body was found to be exactly as it was when it had been buried two years previously without the slightest indication of decomposition. After the customary examination, his body was placed in a new coffin, sealed by ecclesiastical authority and re-buried. In 1921, the relics were transferred to a new cemetery on the mountain near the monastery, and they were transferred again in 1925 to the monastery church. Today, the relics of this young Passionist are still venerated at the Passionist Convent of the Presentation at Mount Argentario.

The decree confirming Galileo's heroic virtue was promulgated in 1981. ✢

14

Gérard Raymond
Canada, 1912–1932

"What Now, Christ?"

Gérard Raymond, a young Canadian boy, seemed to be simply a good and pious student. However, he lived an exceptional interior life. Without going beyond the common order of things in his way of life, he had an intense love of God, a spirit of sacrifice, and an ardent desire for holiness.

―――――

Gérard was born August 20, 1912, in Quebec. He was the fourth of eight children of a streetcar conductor and his wife. Monsieur and Madame Raymond, devout Catholics, gave their children a deep love for Jesus and Mary, for the Eucharist, and for the practice of daily Communion. They taught both by word and example. Charity was a favorite practice of this Christian family. Madame Raymond often made clothes for the poor, and the children were encouraged to donate their savings to those less fortunate. Before Gérard entered school, his mother had taught him his catechism and the practice of daily prayer.

Gérard Raymond

One day when the parish priest came to the Raymond home to pick up some clothing for the poor, he began talking to the lively little Gérard, and questioned him about some parts of the catechism. Apparently, Madame Raymond's lessons had fallen on fertile ground, for the priest, Father Lord, suggested that Gérard be allowed to make his First Communion without delay. Thus, at the age of five-and-a-half, Gérard first met Our Lord in the Eucharist. From then until the end of his brief life, Gérard received Communion almost daily.

Later, at school, he made a pact with a friend: "Every time we pass by a church, we will go in for a minute to visit Jesus. What could make more sense? Jesus is there, our best friend. He's usually alone. He invites us to go in, so why refuse? Some people might call us fools. So be it! We could never take this foolishness further than Jesus, who has hidden himself in the Host for all time, exposing himself to indifference, to scorn, to insults. We will have competed with him in love, but we can never equal him."

At his birth, Madame Raymond consecrated Gérard, as she did all her children, to Our Lady. She followed the pious custom of dressing her babies in nothing but blue and white in honor of the Virgin for the first year of their life. From childhood, Gérard prayed the Rosary, and this devotion became a daily practice for him.

At home, Gérard was happy, affectionate, and always ready to help. In school, Gérard was timid and awkward by temperament. At

Gérard, age three

first, he was seen as distant. He entered the minor seminary of Quebec at the age of twelve. Here, he kept good grades and had a reputation as an excellent student. Very intelligent, he knew how to develop his talents with serious and constant work, so that in 1927 he earned first place in his class.

Outwardly, Gérard Raymond seemed just an ordinary student, if a particularly bright and good one, and a bit reserved. Interiorly, Gérard had immense desires that animated all his actions. At the end of summer vacation in 1929, Gérard wrote to his spiritual director, the Abbé Nadeau: "During my vacation, I never stopped thinking about my vocation. ... Since my childhood, I have never thought about choosing a vocation other than that of the priesthood. ... I want to form in myself a soul that is worthy of receiving the holy anointing, a man worthy to carry Jesus in his hands, to have Him descend upon the altar." Later, he wrote, "I also, I want to practice a whole Christianity. I also, I want to place the cross above every plan, I want to embrace the cross. . . ."

How do we know about the beautiful interior life of this soul? When Gérard was fifteen, he began to keep a little diary. The diary was not written for others to read. He kept it, with the approval of his spiritual director, in order to reflect on his own progress toward God's will. He wrote, ". . . O my God, I wish that this diary would be a long conversation with You, in which I would tell You my sorrows and my joys, and where I would come to renew myself on those days

Gérard at First
Communion, age five

when my fervor is weakened." Although he had ambitions to become a priest and a missionary, he knew the straight path he wished to follow: "Others, the saints, have achieved these heights. I know that I do not deserve this happiness, but I also know, O Jesus, that You want us all to be saints. I know that You are all-powerful, that You created me from nothing, that You are always transforming me with Your grace, that You can still make a saint out of me. Well! Do it; I open myself to You completely, I know very well that You want to make me a saint. *Ad Majorem Dei Gloriam* [All for the greater glory of God]!"

At the annual retreat in 1930, Gérard became consumed with an ardent desire to win souls for God. He wrote, "Help me, O Jesus, to love You more and more. I want to work to become a saint. . . . For some time now, I have felt a constant illness in my body, on the right side. Appendicitis? I don't know. But this pain grips me. . . . Whatever You wish, O my God, do to me what You like. I accept with joy the suffering that You send me; aggravate it if You want, or make it disappear. I give myself entirely to You. . . . O Jesus, I dare to make this wish; accept it if You like, as a witness of my love; if You want, I'm ready. . . . I offer You my life, I sacrifice my life to You, with its dreams of the priesthood and of martyrdom, so that, in exchange, of all the students who are making this retreat with me, not one, not one will be lost for eternity. So that all may love You and work to spread Your kingdom on this earth."

Gérard began to meditate on sacrifice and prayed that he be given the grace to die "just like Jesus, up to the end . . . in the midst of torments, for You, for Your love, and to save souls."

By the end of December, 1931, Gérard was too ill to attend the religious profession of his sister. Although he stayed home, he completed some family chores including installing a new antenna on the roof for the family's radio. In his diary, he reproaches himself for not making better use of his holiday with more prayer and spiritual reading. He writes of his resolutions for the coming year, "I am prepared for all sorrows, all sacrifices that 1932 may bring me. Joyful resignation, conformity to the will of God, that's the least that I can do."

On Saturday, January 2, he wrote the last lines in his diary. "I'm a bit sick again, at the outset of this year; tonight, for the first time in my short life, I spat up a little bit of blood. ... I accept everything, everything, Jesus, in advance ... and I unite everything to Your suffering. I want always to respond with my actions to the question 'What now, Christ?' which is my motto."

Although Gérard returned to the seminary, he only had two days of classes. He began to hemorrhage, and his condition was grave. As he was taken to the hospital, he told his beloved parents, "This is the will of the good God."

In the hospital, Gérard remained calm and serene. On June 16, he asked for extreme unction, and all who were there testified as to the joy that radiated from him on receiving the sacrament. He died peacefully during the night of July 5.

Gérard, age thirteen, at the minor seminary of Quebec

In the weeks following Gérard's death, his mother found his diary among his effects. She had not known all the secrets of her son's soul. Mrs. Raymond showed the diary to the priests of the archdiocesan seminary of Quebec who recognized the work as that of a specially favored soul. Some extracts were published and his reputation for holiness began to spread. A cause for his beatification is being studied in the Diocese of Quebec. ✣

15

Blessed Karolina Kózka
Poland, 1898–1914

Martyr for Purity

Deep in the woods, only the birds and small creatures heard the young girl's screams. The silver bayonet flashed in the sunlight as it slashed again and again at this foolish girl who would not give in to the soldier's dark desires. His anger is proved by the marks on the body. At last, the screams stopped and the girl's body lay, bleeding and lifeless, at the mercy of the weather and natural predators.

Meanwhile, in the small Polish village of Wal-Ruda, her frantic parents and fellow villagers searched for young Karolina Kózka. She was known as a "real angel," a good and devout girl, and they knew she would not have left home voluntarily or without saying where she was going.

Two village children saw her on November 18, 1914, being led by a Russian soldier. Where? No one knew. At last, sixteen days later, the broken body was found. The pathetic corpse with its grisly wounds told a tale of heroic resistance; both hands held up in protest had been cut to the bone; she was wounded in the head, shoulder, and knee, and her throat was slit. Karolina had become one of the countless victims of the Russian occupation of Poland.

———

Karolina Kózka was born August 2, 1898, the eighth of the eleven children of Jan and Maria Borzecka Kózka. The family lived in a devout rural community where Karolina was raised as a true daughter of the Church.

The villagers called the Kózka home "the little church." An apostolic spirit was a family trait. Karolina often invited neighbors and relatives over to read the Bible as a group, or to listen to readings from the lives of the saints and other Catholic literature. At Christmas, they would join in singing the traditional carols of the season, and during Lent they sang the Passion of the Lord. A spirit of love of God and duty to neighbor prevailed in this Christian home. The entire family prayed in common before meals and in the evening, and they sang the little office of the Blessed Virgin each day. They attended Mass on Sundays and, when possible, on weekdays as well.

From childhood, Karolina loved to pray. Often during the day, she would quietly say the Hail Mary, saying she loved it "because it makes me feel a great joy in my heart." She was especially devoted to the Rosary. At night, she often prayed until very late. Karolina also loved her country and never ceased to pray fervently for its liberty.

Karolina's uncle, Frederick Borzecki, was an inspiration for the religious and cultural life of the village. A third-order Franciscan, he served as a deacon for the parish. Karolina worked with him, helping in the library and in the room where the town meetings were held.

Karolina was sensitive to the needs of her neighbors, and often helped the elderly and the sick with small chores. She served as a catechist for her younger brothers and sisters and for the other children of the area as well. One of these children later testified during the beatification process. The child's own mother had died when she was quite young, and she said that Karolina was "more than a mother to me."

Symbolic painting of Karolina used at her beatification

To others, Karolina seemed reserved, somewhat quiet and self disciplined. At sixteen, she was attractive and enthusiastic about life and her future. That future was cut short by the attack of a Russian soldier when she resisted his advances.

The heroic martyr of purity was buried two days after her body was discovered. She was laid to rest in a parish plot at her parish, Sabawa. Soon the people of the region began to venerate her, and she was honored with the title "Star of the People." The sturdy Polish

Catholics spontaneously came together to pray both at the site of her martyrdom and at her tomb. In 1917, her remains were solemnly transferred from the parochial cemetery to a special tomb erected on the side of the parish church. A cross was erected at the site of her martyrdom. The route from her home to the place of her murder is marked with the Stations of the Cross.

Today, her relics rest in a beautiful bronze reliquary. A beautiful stained glass window in the church is a gift from Polish-American emigrants who were former inhabitants of the region of Tarnow in Southern Poland.

Because of the sad political situation, the light of this young Polish girl shone only in her own country for many years. The cause for her beatification began in 1965. Declared a martyr for purity, Karolina was beatified by Pope John Paul II during his third pastoral visit to his native country in 1987. Her feast day was established as November 18, the day of her death.

The only known photo of Karolina is taken from a group photo made at her school in 1913, when she was fifteen years old. ✛

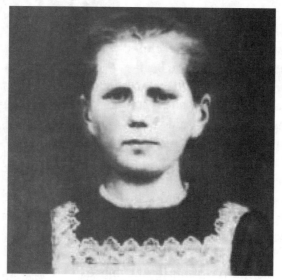

Actual photo of Karolina

16

Blessed Laura Vicuña
Chile & Argentina, 1891–1904

Willing Young Victim for Love

Beaten and bruised, the young girl was dying of severe internal injuries. Her mother and the Salesian sisters stood by her bedside, praying and keeping watch with her. It was time to tell her secret. As her mother leaned close, Laura whispered, "Mama, I'm dying, but I'm happy to offer my life for you. I asked Our Lord for this."

Stunned, Mercedes Vicuña fell to her knees sobbing. She realized what her daughter meant, and begged Laura's forgiveness as well as the forgiveness of God. She promised to begin her life again.

––––––––

Laura Vicuña was born in Santiago, Chile, on April 5, 1891. Her father was a soldier who belonged to a noble Chilean family, and her mother, Mercedes, was a simple country girl. Mr. Vicuña's family never fully accepted his marriage to a wife who they felt was beneath his station.

A revolution and civil war had broken out the previous January, and Mr. Vicuña carried Mercedes and Laura into political exile in the Andes Mountains. Still an infant, Laura was in poor health and her neighbors feared she would die or be handicapped. However, by the time she was eighteen months old, she was thriving.

Shortly before Laura's third birthday, and after the birth of her baby sister Julia, Mr. Vicuña died, leaving his widow to care for the children. Mercedes took the girls to the frontier town of Las Lajas, where she hoped to find work as a cook and laundry woman. There she met Manuel Mora, owner of a large ranch. Mr. Mora offered to be her protector, and his financial support would pay tuition for the girls at the newly formed missionary school run by the Salesian sisters (Daughters of Mary Help of Christians). In return for his help and protection, Mercedes became his mistress.

When Laura was eight, Mercedes, on the advice of one of the Salesian missionary priests, took both girls to board at the school in Junín. Life at the school was very pleasant. Laura said, "I certainly was happy to go to Junín. I think the Infant Jesus was glad, and gave me this feeling of joy, so much alive and so new to me."

Sister Angela, the superior, took Laura to show her the school chapel. She later wrote, "As soon as Laura entered, she looked at 'Jesus' little house,' as she called the tabernacle, and when she was told that Jesus lived there she blew him a kiss and promised to come back often."

Here Laura learned about God and His love, and learned to repay this love with love for her fellow students and the sisters. Laura was a leader in sports and a friend to all. She helped the younger children with their daily tasks, such as making their beds, and with their personal chores, such as combing their hair or mending their clothes. She acted as peacemaker for the children's quarrels. When her little sister Julia was naughty, Laura gently corrected her.

Everyone looked up to Laura. She was serious and wise beyond her age. She had a mature understanding of prayer and, because she was a natural leader, she seemed to build up a joyful spirit of piety in all her fellow students. "Wherever I am, at school, at play, or anywhere else, the thought of God accompanies me, helps me, and consoles me," she said.

On her first summer vacation at home, Laura began to realize the type of life her mother was leading. In addition, Mr. Mora was often drunk. At these times he would attempt to embrace and kiss Laura, who was repelled by his advances and his whiskey-laden breath. Laura's mother demanded that he leave the child alone, which he did except when he was drunk. At these times Laura made every effort to keep out of his way.

Laura made her First Communion when she was ten. This was a decisive moment in her life, and she wrote in her notebook, "O my God, I want to love You and serve You all my life. I give You my soul, my heart, my whole self."

Mercedes came to Junín for the festive occasion, but Laura noticed that her mother did not receive the Sacrament. She seemed to realize that her mother was not happy. One of her constant prayers before the tabernacle became, "Jesus, I wish that Mama would know You better and be happy."

In December of that same year, Laura was enrolled in the sodality of the Children of Mary. The medal of the sodality, which she wore constantly, was not just a symbol but, it seemed to her, a protective shield.

Laura was fascinated by the devotion of the sisters. They had courageously left their home countries to dedicate their lives to the service of God in the missions of Patagonia. Laura secretly hoped one day to follow their example and become a sister herself. She said, "I want to do all I can to make God known and loved." She prayed, "My God, I want to love and serve You all my life."

When Laura was eleven, Bishop John Cagliero made a visit to the school. Laura asked him if she could become a Salesian sister. Laughingly, he replied, "Just wait a little longer, child." But Laura did not want to wait. Repeatedly she asked her confessor to pray and ask God if it was His will for her to become a Salesian. This understanding priest agreed that she did, in truth, have a religious vocation, but it remained their secret. She wrote, "My God, give me a life of loving service, of mortification, of sacrifice."

Blessed Laura Vicuña

In the summer of 1901, Laura again returned to the ranch for summer vacation. Mr. Mora seemed more than ever to be becoming quite interested in her, fawning and fussing over her. Through prayer and vigilance she determined to protect her purity. "Lord, do not let me offend You," she prayed.

One day, the moment she had feared finally arrived; she was caught alone with Mr. Mora. He began to make improper advances, and she struggled ferociously, finally breaking away and running outdoors. She knew, however, that he would not give up, and at a fiesta a few days later, he approached her and asked her for a dance. Laura flatly refused in spite of Mr. Mora's threats and her mother's entreaties.

Laura spent that night hiding outside in the dark, while Mr. Mora vented his anger on her hapless mother. For revenge, he refused to continue paying Laura's tuition at school, but the sisters heard of the matter and offered to accept the girls free. Embarrassed at this charitable offer, Mercedes sent only Laura back to school, keeping Julia at home with herself.

On Easter 1902, Laura was confirmed by Bishop Cagliero. She realized that she had not offered the supreme sacrifice for her mother, and begged her confessor, Father Crestanello, to be allowed to offer her life to God for her mother's conversion. After talking with Laura, the priest realized that he was dealing with a soul who had been given great spiritual gifts, and he gave her permission to make the offering.

During the winter of 1903, Laura became ill. Her mother begged her to come home with her, and the superior told Laura, "Your mother needs you more than you need her. You must go."

At the ranch, Laura's health steadily worsened, instead of improving with the better climate and good care. She felt that her offering had been accepted, and did not believe she would ever get well.

At first, Mr. Mora stayed out on the range most of the time. But when he returned, Laura noticed that he had cooled towards her mother, and he looked at Laura with a strange desire, especially when drunk. Mercedes also noticed his attitude and, in spite of his threats, she packed up with the girls and rented a small place in Junín.

The night of January 14, 1904, Mr. Mora, drunk with whiskey, anger, and lust, rode into town and announced his intention of spending the night at the cottage where Mercedes and the girls were staying. Whip in hand, he demanded that Mercedes accede to his wishes and that his "family" return the following day to the ranch with him.

Weak and pale, Laura resolutely announced, "If he stays, I will go." She did not wait for an answer, but walked out the door. Mr. Mora was furious. He followed her outside and Mercedes screamed for Laura to run. Laura attempted to run for safety to the sisters' residence, but Mr. Mora caught her in the street. He whipped her and kicked her as she lay in the street crying for help. When some men ran out of nearby houses, Mora picked the girl up and tried to put her across his horse. Then, realizing the danger, he tossed her, unconscious, back into the street and rode away.

Laura lingered for a week, as her mother and the sisters kept watch over her. Father Crestanello, her confessor, came and heard Laura's confession and gave her absolution. He had questions, but Laura simply told him that she forgave her attacker and bore him no ill will.

On January 21, Laura and her younger sister were alone. Laura earnestly made a request of her sister, who later wrote down from memory the words Laura said to her. "Be good to Mama, don't give her trouble; respect her always. Don't ever leave her, even if later on you will have a family of your own. Don't look down upon the poor, but be kind to them. Love Our Lord and the Blessed Virgin. Pray every day to your guardian angel to keep you from sin. Don't forget, Julia, we will be together in heaven." The next morning, a Salesian missionary brought Laura communion and gave her the last rites.

When Laura and her mother were alone, Laura revealed her secret. Laura passed quietly from this world, happy with her mother's promise to repent. After Laura's death at about six o'clock in the evening of January 22, 1904, Mercedes went to the chapel and made her confession. Through the witness of her courageous daughter, she returned to the practice of the Faith.

When Pope John Paul II beatified Laura on September 3, 1988, he called her the "Eucharistic flower of Junín de Los Andes," whose life was a poem of purity, sacrifice, and filial love." ✧

17

Lucas da Rocha Silva
Brazil, 1994–2003

One Small Boy; One Large Example

Holding an image of the child Jesus and a Miraculous Medal in his little hands, a young boy breathed his last, and his soul left to celebrate its first Christmas in heaven.

Lucas da Rocha Silva was born November 28, 1994, in Itaquera, a neighborhood in an industrial area of São Paulo. Lucas was the second son of Carlos Alberto Gil da Silva and Aparecida da Rocha Silva. Mr. da Silva worked in administration for a decorating company that specialized in arranging festivals. Aparecida was a nurse's aid in a cardiology clinic at the municipal hospital of Tatuape. He had one older brother, Klayton. A strong Catholic family, the da Rochas were devoted to *Nossa Senhora Aparecida*, the patroness of Brazil, and visited her shrine there three times each year. On the first anniversary of their marriage, Aparecida went to the sanctuary to bring her wedding clothes as a gift to the Virgin, to fulfill a promise she had made on her wedding day.

Lucas grew as a normal child, happy and lively, until he was nearly six years old. On the early morning of November 1, 2000, he woke up with an extreme pain in the shinbone of his left leg. From that time, he began to walk a painful Way of the Cross that providence, in its mysterious design, had reserved for him, and which he accepted in an exemplary way until his death on December 15, 2003.

X-rays indicated a bone fracture in the locality of the pain which the doctors began to treat. After a month, however, instead of getting better, the pain began to increase. Although the leg was put in a cast, the pain continued. Lucas began to pray the Hail Mary at night, "until the pain passes," he said, in order to be able to sleep a little, but the following day the pain would begin again.

In March of 2001, a biopsy made at the Hospital Santa Marcelina indicated a tumor in the bone, and Lucas was taken to the Institute of Pediatric Oncology of the São Paulo Hospital. He received a bone implant to try and stop the tumor's growth, but it expanded into the knee and then into the femur, which led to two surgeries, the last of which, in April 2003, resulted in the amputation of his left leg.

Although just a child, Lucas accepted all of his suffering as the will of God, with a mature and admirable Christian spirit, without complaining of his pain or misfortune. This willing acceptance was witnessed by all who knew him.

During the nearly three years of his illness, Lucas suffered continuously. Once he asked his mother, "Mom, why did I come into the world to suffer so much?" She explained that God had asked that of him, and so he was to accept it. He then asked, if he had been born first, would his brother have had the illness. When she told him no, he said that he understood, and he accepted his cross without rebellion. All his subsequent actions showed his serenity in this acceptance.

At the beginning of his illness, Lucas had received some counseling at the hospital about the nature of his disease. On his seventh birthday, he wrote in his notebook:

"I am a fighter, and God will give me strength. I am strong and God will help me in my walk (in this life). God, you help me so much, and the hospital is very good and they will help me a great deal also. I hope I am going to win this battle. I thank God for my existence."

Lucas at the age of seven

After the treatment with chemotherapy, Lucas lost most of his hair. His brother told him that if he had lost his hair, he would never leave the house. Lucas responded, "That is foolish! I am still the same person I was."

From the time of his first surgery, Lucas had to get up very early three times each week to go to the hospital to be examined and to have sessions of chemotherapy and radiotherapy. While waiting there, he visited with the others in a lively and cheerful manner, participating in games and encouraging the other children with similar illnesses. He cheered them up when they were depressed and sad. Sometimes, when the wait at the hospital was a long one, he would tell the doctor,

"Aunt, please tell them to call me soon, because I need to go to school." (In Brazil, when speaking to an older woman, children do not use official titles such as "Doctor," but rather use the familiar yet respectful term "Aunt." Likewise, they would call a man "Uncle.")

Lucas had a sense of duty about his education which he kept until the end. At school, he worked hard and his marks were always good. When he was only five, he asked his parents to help him open a savings account in a bank so that he could save the money necessary to pay for his later education. He put the money he received as gifts into his account, and by the time of his death he had accumulated a substantial amount toward this goal.

Lucas was, by nature, neat and orderly. In his coloring book, he colored with balance and harmony. At the hospital, in the playroom for children, he colored various small pictures which he gave to his grandmother. He completed the most recent one only about ten days before his death and gave it to his parents. It, too, was done with care, order, and equilibrium.

Even after his leg had been amputated, Lucas continued to play ball with his friends on the patio of his home. He often played the position of goalie, defending the arch. His parents say that when playing with the other children, he never became agitated as children often do. He did not become depressed with the afflictions he endured because of his condition.

Lucas also continued to ride his beloved bicycle with the aid of a special pedal and strap. He would place the bike against the wall or the grill by the entrance to the house in order to mount it, and did the same thing to stop.

From April of 2003, in spite of all the best medical care and treatments, the tumor continued to grow, spreading from his leg bone to his lungs, his jaw, and his neck, multiplying his sufferings. He began to have difficulties speaking, eating, and even breathing.

In September of 2003, while Lucas was waiting for the interminable exams and treatments, an acquaintance gave him a medal of Our Lady of Grace — the Miraculous Medal. As the medal was slipped around his neck, Lucas looked as proud as if he were a soldier receiving a decoration for bravery. He treasured the gift with sincere piety, keeping it to the last moments of his short life, which was already fading. He also treasured a little book about Our Lady of Fátima and the three little seers. He especially liked knowing that Jacinta also died as a young child near his own age, and each night he asked his mother to read to him from the book. Afterwards, he prayed the Guardian Angel prayer and the Hail Mary before going to sleep.

A few weeks before Christmas, Lucas was given a small image of the child Jesus in the manger, which he received with devotion and joy, serenely telling his parents that this Christmas he would go to Jesus in heaven and join his paternal grandmother who had died a few months before. In November, the chemotherapy and radiotherapy treatments were suspended because his little body could not endure them any longer.

His parents called their family and friends to the church of Saint John Bosco near their home and announced that the doctors could do nothing more. Lucas was now in the hands of God and Our Lady. Sitting near the altar, Lucas heard the announcement with the same uncomplaining Christian serenity and resignation that he had kept since the beginning of his illness.

On December 9, Lucas received a beautiful surprise. During Mass at his parish church, at the time for Communion, Carlos Alberto carried Lucas in his arms to the altar as he went to receive. The parish priest gave Communion to Carlos, and then, as his First Communion, to Lucas who, with no prior warning, received Our Lord seriously and joyfully.

The night of December 13, his respiratory problems worsened, and Lucas was rushed to the hospital. In the little desk in his room he left, arranged in perfect order, the holy cards of his favorite saints: Mary Help of Christians, Saint John Bosco, Saint Paulina, Blessed Fray Galvão, Saint Rita of Cascia, Saint Benedict, and the novena of Our Lady of Grace. He took with him his two most valuable treasures, his miraculous medal and the little statue of the child Jesus. On Sunday the 14th, he received the last sacrament from his parish priest. The following day, with extreme difficulty of breathing, he entered his final agony. He remained conscious, tightly holding the medal and little statue. When he felt his strength leaving him, he managed with great difficulty to whisper, "Mama, help me to hold the child Jesus." A little later, he breathed his last. Without a doubt, the child Jesus repaid the affection of this innocent little soul, carrying it with Him to spend its first Christmas in heaven.

In the photo used on his memorial card, Lucas is dressed in the uniform of the race car driver Airton Senna. Senna is one of the most popular Brazilian racers in the Formula One. The uniform was a gift of his parents, along with a little miniature car with a motor which Lucas raced around the patio of his home and at his grandmother's home in the country.

The text of the card, written by his parents, reads:

Memorial card of Lucas

There was no greater blessing
Than his existence,
Whether in a perfect body
Or a body deformed.
That it is worthwhile to live
Is already confirmed.
We thank the Creator
For the moments lived
As a way of love
He granted to him.
He gave the best of himself
In each place he passed
And he never forgot
That it is worthwhile
To fight!

Lucas was buried in the cemetery of Itaquera. Those who have visited there to pray and to pay their respect have reported a marked environment of peace and serenity at his grave.

Often, there are anonymous souls whose heroism is known to God alone. Other times, He shows us a heroic soul for our edification, and to help us, by their good example, to face our own daily crosses. At the tender age of nine, Lucas was a hero because of his faith and his complete acceptance of the mysterious and luminous road of pain that providence deigned he walk, following the steps of the Divine Teacher. Small in size, little Lucas is a big example for all of us. ✝

18

Venerable Mari Carmen González-Valero
Spain, 1930–1939

The Power of Pardon

November 3, 1940, Manuel Azana, former anticlerical president of the Spanish Republic, died while in exile in France. According to the bishop who assisted him, he received the sacrament of penance while fully aware, and died reconciled to the God he had tried to eradicate from Spain. Undoubtedly, he was unaware that he had crossed paths with a nine-year-old child who prayed and suffered for him. Today, that same child is on her way to the altars of the Catholic Church. She was declared venerable in 1996.

Mari Carmen González-Valero's father was executed during the dark days of religious persecution at the start of the Spanish Civil War. She had pardoned her father's murderers, and their salvation was her great preoccupation. In the mind of this young girl, Manuel Azana, the president of the Republic, became the symbol of her father's assassins. She asked her mother if Azana would be saved, and her mother replied that if he were repentant and if she prayed for him, he would. From that time, she began to pray daily for the conversion of her father's murderers. She told her aunt, "Aunt Fifa, let us pray for Papa and for those who killed him." According to this aunt, with whom Mari Carmen lived for a time, the child prayed the Rosary of the Divine Wounds for this intention every day. Later, when she became ill, she offered her sufferings for her father and those who killed him. She told her nurse, "My father died a martyr, poor Mama, and I am dying a victim."

———

Mari Carmen was the second child of Don Julio González-Valero and Doña Carmen Saenz de Heredia, a deeply religious couple. Don Julio was an engineer for a railroad; Doña Carmen was a housewife who attended scrupulously to the Christian upbringing of her five children. The couple consecrated their child to the Virgin of Carmen before Mari Carmen was born, and a number of times afterwards when they visited Marian shrines. Dona Carmen made, and kept, a vow to dress the baby in blue and white in honor of the virgin until the baby was three years old.

When Mari Carmen was born on March 14, 1930, she became gravely ill and was baptized immediately in her own home. The tiny baby was named Maria del Carmen Gonzáles-Valero y Saenz de Heredia. The sick child recovered, and her constitution became unusually strong; physically, she was very well developed for her age.

The Papal Nuncio in Spain, Msgr. Federico Tedeschini, was a friend of the family. In 1932, he administered the sacrament of confirmation in Hortaleza and invited the González-Valeros to bring their children. Thus, Mari Carmen was confirmed on April 16 at the tender age of two years. Although confirmation at such a young age seems unusual now, this was the custom at the time in Spain.

From the time she was a small girl, Mari Carmen was distinguished by an extreme sensitivity with regard to purity. Her grandmother says she had an "instinctive modesty which comes from God." Later, her nurse testified that even with the suffocating heat she never asked to remove any of her clothes and asked for her injections to be put in a place which was more painful but more modest.

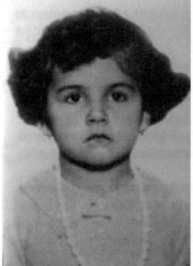

A long name for such a little girl: Maria del Carmen González-Valero y Saenz de Heredia

Mari Carmen was also remarkable for her charity. If a poor person came to the door and she was the one who answered, she would give them alms from her own savings and tell them, "Come again and my mother will give you something." While at school in Zalla, she directed that all of the gifts she received on Three Kings Day be given to the poor, which they were. A few days before her final illness, she wrote to her grandmother asking for some wool to knit a sweater for

Mari Carmen at six months with her mother

the poor. She once told her mother, "Mama, you must treat the servants well. It is enough that they are serving us. Remember that you, too, are a servant, because you serve God." Her grandmother testified that when she was given money for toys, Mari Carmen would give it to the landlady to buy toys for her children, telling her not to tell her mother or grandmother what she had done. Once, the child found the governess crying because she had no family and therefore no one wrote to her. From time to time after that Mari Carmen would write her letters, pretending she was an old friend. The governess knew what was going on, of course, but pretended that she didn't because, as she said, "her letters were so helpful that nothing could take their place."

Honesty, too, was a hallmark of this little Spanish girl. Her grandmother said that she never remembered Mari Carmen telling a lie. Once, having been told a white lie by her mother, Mari Carmen told her, "Please, always tell me the truth and I won't be upset, but do not lie, Mama."

Mari Carmen's grandmother, also named Carmen, ran a small office from her home to promote devotion to the Heart of Jesus Most Merciful. Mari Carmen gave her grandmother money from her savings to buy promotional literature for distribution. Even in revolutionary Madrid, Mari Carmen would sometimes go out and distribute literature and holy pictures to passers-by.

In spite of her piety and her goodness, Mari Carmen was a normal little girl who loved to play with dolls and who begged for sweets. She had an alert mind, a lively intelligence, and a strong will. She was simple and natural in her manner and disliked pretensions.

After her older brother received First Communion, Mari Carmen began to beg her mother to be allowed to receive also. She made her First Communion on June 27, 1936, when she was six years old. Although six was a young age for this sacrament at the time, her mother says, "I was convinced that we were going to face hard times in Spain and in our own family in the face of the religious persecution which was about to take place, and I wanted so much for the child to receive her Lord before that should happen." The Spanish Civil war began only days later.

Just over a month later, Communist militants took Mari Carmen's father before a terrorist tribunal. Full of foreboding, Julio told his wife, "The children are all small now and they do not understand; but when they are older tell them that their father fought and gave his life for God and for Spain so that they can be educated in a Catholic Spain, with the Crucified One presiding in the schools." Julio was released that same day, possibly so he could consider the invitation to serve again in the army, this time on the side of the Republic. He was taken again a few days later. His family was able to see him for only a few moments each day as they passed in front of the prison. On August 29, Doña Carmen heard a voice calling her name from a truck that was passing by. A little while later her husband was shot.

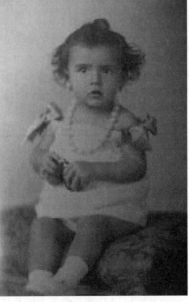

At age one

The danger seemed grave for Doña Carmen because of her noble relatives, and she sought asylum in the Belgian embassy. The children remained with their Aunt Sofia. Mari Carmen's older brother was terrified that his mother would be killed when they left her at the embassy, but Mari Carmen understood and took his arm, calming him as she led him home. Seeing the fears of her aunt, Mari Carmen told her, "Don't be upset. Let's say the Rosary and recall Jesus' wounds."

The family received notice that the children, along with many others, were to be taken to Russia to be educated in Marxism. The Belgian ambassador agreed to bring the children to the embassy, although there was barely room for them. On February 11, the children went to the embassy with six-year-old Mari Carmen carrying her baby sister in her arms. Only minutes after they left their house, a military truck arrived to take the children.

Although Mari Carmen helped her mother very much, she did get in her mother's bad graces once. When her mother saw the large doll which Mari Carmen had begged the ambassador to bring from her house, she angrily chided the child for her foolishness in bothering the ambassador about such a thing. Although she was pious and very good, Mari Carmen was a normal little girl and the doll was one of her prized possessions.

On March 31, 1937, the embassy organized an evacuation for the González-Valero family. They traveled to Valencia in trucks, then by boat to Marseilles, France, and from there to San Sebastian in nationalist Spain. Here, Mari Carmen first attended a school run by the Religious of the Sacred Heart, and then transferred to a boarding school run by Irish nuns in Zalla.

At Zalla, Mari Carmen showed a great interest in the missions. She worked to promote one of the school's organizations dedicated to them, and saved her pennies to give on *DOMUND*, the Sunday when a special collection is taken for the Society of the Propagation of the Faith to support missions. According to her religion teacher, she also offered childish little mortifications for the missions. One day, after she made the spiritual exercises with the students and had gone in the garden to play with her friends, the priest who had directed the retreat spoke to one of the nuns. "Tell me Mother, who is that dark girl whose name is Carmencita?" The sister pointed her out, "There she is right now, Father, running across the garden." The priest commented, "That child is filled with the Holy Spirit!"

On Holy Thursday, April 6, 1939, Mari Carmen went to Mass with her grandmother at the Good Shepherd Church in San Sebastian. Here, she made her total surrender to God. She asked her grandmother, "What does it mean to surrender oneself?" The pious grandmother answered her, "To surrender oneself is to give oneself entirely to God and to belong entirely to God." Mari Carmen then asked if she should surrender herself and her grandmother answered in the affirmative. Her grandmother recalls that after Communion that day, Mari Carmen spent a long time on her knees giving thanks.

After Mass, Mari Carmen asked her grandmother to take her to a bakery where she invited everyone in the place to have some pastry. The contrast between her angelic deportment during Mass and the immediate demand for sweets somewhat annoyed her grandmother, who later said, "I didn't realize that she really wanted to celebrate something. I thought to myself, 'just like a child!'"

Later, it was discovered that one of the entries in Mari Carmen's diary says that her parents would celebrate the Lord's day by buying pastries after Mass. In her childish way, then, Mari Carmen was celebrating the spiritual importance she attributed to that day, as well as her inner joy, rather than satisfying the demands of a sweet tooth.

When Mari Carmen returned to school, an epidemic of scarlet fever appeared among the student body. By May 8, she was put to bed, ill. She returned home, and at first the illness did not seem to be serious, but it soon became complicated by an infection of the ear and the mastoid. Septicemia set in and settled in her heart and kidneys. On May 27 she was taken to Madrid for an operation. She suffered untold agonies with great patience and an admirable love of God until the Virgin took her to herself on July 17, 1939.

When her grandmother asked her to join in a novena for her recovery, Mari Carmen answered, "Let happen what God wants, as Mother Annunciata used to say." When her mother asked her to ask the Child Jesus to cure her, she replied, "No, Mama, I don't ask for that. I ask that His will be done."

Mari Carmen had her secrets. She kept a small diary. In her childish script,

Dressed for an outing to the beach

she had written three times at the beginning and the end of the book "private." The book was kept in an envelope sealed with adhesive paper, also marked "private, private, private," inside her school bag. After her death, the envelope was discovered, and in it we are able to read her great secret: "I surrendered myself in the parish church of the Good Shepherd, April 6, 1939."

Once, during her illness, Mari Carmen noticed her mother burdened with domestic work and said to her, "Mama, you worry too much about the things of earth. You should pray more. We are only on a journey." Her mother answered, "Child, I have to keep the house in order." Mari Carmen responded, "Mama, your home is in heaven. Mama, when you are on a trip and you stay in a hotel, you do not worry about fixing up the room and you do not hang up Papa's picture. The night does not pass in any special way. That, Mama, is life. That is the way of this world."

Although at least one of her doctors knew it was an impossible situation from the outset, they did not cease to try every possible remedy, no matter how painful. Mari Carmen bore the agony of her martyrdom with uncomplaining resignation, often begging pardon when she could not repress a cry of pain. "You, doctor, and everybody, excuse me." During these sufferings, so excessive for a little child, she did not cease to love God. A number of times she asked her mother to sing the hymn she remembered from her First Communion, with its refrain of "Jesus, I want to love you with all my heart, how good you are, how good you are."

From the beginning of her illness, Mari Carmen predicted her death, although at first no one paid attention because it did not seem to be a serious ailment. Later, she said the Virgin would come to fetch her on her feast day, July 16. When she learned that this was the day her Aunt Sofia was to be married, she did not want to interfere with the festivities and announced she would die the following day. Her aunt visited her the day before her marriage and promised to bring the flowers from her wedding. "No, Aunt Sofia, just send me the lilies. I am going to need them."

On the morning of the 17th, Mari Carmen sat up in bed, a thing she had not been able to do for some time, and said, "Today I am going to die. Today I am going to heaven!" Although she seemed better, her mother, seeing Mari Carmen's fervor, called the entire family. After making an act of contrition, Mari Carmen told her mother in a sweet, natural voice, "Mama, very soon I am going to see Papa. Do you have a message for him?" As her mother dissolved in tears, Mari Carmen kissed her and said, "Don't be upset, Mama, I will pray for you." Then she began to speak of Jesus the Good Shepherd, and her mother thought she was delirious, but her grandmother told Dona Carmen to think of the beautiful things Mari Carmen was telling them. A few moments before dying, she looked at her relatives gathered around her bed and said, "Love one another."

Mari Carmen seemed to hear singing and celestial music, and told her doctor, "Leave me alone, Doctor. Let me go. Don't you see that the Virgin is coming with angels to fetch me?"

About three o'clock in the afternoon, Mari Carmen pronounced her final words, "Jesus, Mary, and Joseph, assist me in my last agony. Jesus, Mary, and Joseph, grant that when I

At the age of five, with her younger brother, dressed as little Dutch children

die, I die in peace and my soul comes to be with you." She sat up a little and then fell back on her pillow, dying quietly and without any agony.

When Mari Carmen died, she was disfigured and deformed by the ravages of her illness. One of her uncles first noticed that there had been a change. Her nurse testified, "Before she died she was all stiff and smelled bad. She had septicemia and colitis and, as much as we tried to cleanse her, she gave off a bad odor. When she died, I was impressed by her complete change. She gave off a sweet aroma, a fragrance that came from her and not from the flowers that they put around her. Her stiffness disappeared and she became entirely flexible."

They dressed Mari Carmen in her white First Communion dress and laid her among the lilies from her aunt's wedding. On the evening of that hot day, Dr. Blanco Soler later testified that he urged them to

"The best adornment for a child is virtue" – Mari Carmen

remove the flowers and put them in water to keep them fresh for the burial. Her mother removed some of them, but left a few around Mari Carmen's face. The following morning, all the flowers that stayed in place were covered with a mysterious mist and seemed as if they had just been cut, while the flowers in water were withered. For the forty-eight hours until she was buried, she showed no signs of rigidity, her color and general appearance remained lovely, and the lilies around her remained fresh.

Her brother Julio says that her reputation for sanctity began shortly after her death and precisely among those who had seen her die. The diocesan process for her cause for beatification began on July 11, 1961. In 1972, Mari Carmen's mortal remains were transferred to the church of the Monastery of the Discacled Carmelites in Aravaca, a suburb of Madrid. Mari Carmen González-Valero was declared venerable January 12, 1996.

One day soon we may be able to call Mari Carmen González-Valero, this child who understood the power of pardon and who so generously gave herself to God, blessed. ✣

19

Saint Maria Teresa Goretti
Italy, 1890-1902

Martyr for Purity

"No! No! No! What are you doing? Do not touch me! It is a sin! You will go to hell!" Eleven-year-old Maria Goretti struggled to repulse the sexual advances of the husky, nineteen year old Alessandro Serenelli. He pushed a handkerchief into her mouth to stifle her cries. Although his brute strength could easily have overcome her resistance, somehow the force of will in the young girl's eyes stopped him and he could not rape her. Instead, he brought out a sharp knife and began stabbing her, mortally wounding her. She fell in a pool of her own blood and he stamped off into his room and slammed the door.

Before this final dramatic refusal, Maria had several times resisted blandishments and threats from Alessandro. The canonization of Maria Goretti was not based on a single moment's struggle, however, but upon her practice of heroic virtue throughout her entire short life.

Maria's story begins with her home, where the moral basis of her heroic choice was nurtured. Her mother, Assunta, was an orphan who had never learned to read or write. Maria's father served in the military, then returned to his home town of Corinaldo, Italy, married Assunta, and began to farm for a living. The couple had little to sustain them other than their love for God, Our Lady, and each other.

Although Assunta had never been to school for any formal lessons, she learned from the Church about the love of God, and transmitted this great love, by words and actions, to her family. Luigi, her husband, also had a deep love and devotion to God. Rather than feel bitter about their lack of material things, this valiant couple accepted everything as God's will, and greeted the birth of each of their children as a great gift from God. The lesson of love was imparted to each child. After the death of their first son as an infant, Luigi and Assunta had another boy, and on October 16, 1890, Asunta gave birth to a girl.

In thanksgiving, the child was named Maria, after Our Lady, and Teresa, after the great saint of Carmel. She was baptized the day after her birth. Later, Maria and her brother were also confirmed in Corinaldo according to the custom of the time when children were confirmed at a young age, before their First Communion.

The family grew to four children, and the poverty, which had never been absent, became acute. In Corinaldo, the family had a small house and plot of land. Although Luigi managed the land well, it simply was not large enough to raise an adequate supply of food. The family had few possessions, and a small image of Our Lady was considered their greatest treasure. The children had no toys, so an apple or rock often took the place of the ball another child might have played with. Maria never had a single doll. Because of their poverty, the children never attended school. But in spite of everything, the entire family was happy, until the food shortage became so critical that something had to be done.

Luigi and Assunta loved their small home in this beautiful part of Italy. To better their fortune, however, they decided to become tenant farmers in a different part of the country. They realized the needs of the children might be better met by this move. As Luigi explained it, "We must not think of ourselves; but they [the children] are gifts from the good God and we must show our gratitude by taking care of them."

At the age of six, her father credited Maria's mother with having taught her to be obedient, to pray well, and to love God and His Blessed Mother. Like other children her age, she played, running through the grass, picking flowers, and smiling. Her mother tells us that even by this age Maria began to have an understanding beyond her years. Maria was obedient, but rather than waiting to be asked to help, she begged to be allowed the privilege. She enjoyed playing, but most often she played with her younger brothers to amuse them and keep them from bothering their mother. Cheerfulness is the one thing that all who knew her mentioned when giving testimony for her beatification.

When Maria was eight, the family moved to the Pontine. Although much of this land has now been reclaimed through reforms, in Maria's day it was one of the grimmest parts of Italy. Because of the swamps, disease was rampant — especially diseases carried by mosquitoes. Even the air there was said to be unhealthy. Maria's father, along with his partner, Signor Serenelli, and Serenelli's sixteen-year-old son, Alessandro, became tenant farmers to Conte Mazzoleni.

At Ferriere di Conca, the Gorettis and the Serenellis moved together into housing above an old dairy barn. Previously, Luigi had expressed concern as to the effect the atmosphere would have on the children, but Assunta had predicted that Maria would be their joy wherever she was. True to this prediction, Maria remained a happy, helpful child. Because of her exceptional goodness, she was loved by all who knew here. She was a pretty girl with long, light chestnut hair.

Although she was always clean and neat, vanity had no part in her personality.

Saint Maria Goretti icon by Rev. William Hart McNichols

Many of Maria's friends wore roses in their hair in the absence of jewelry or lace. One day the landowner was on a tour of inspection and noticed this young girl who wore no flower in her hair. He asked the foreman to bring her over and after a few remarks she was sent back to her play with the other children. The foreman spoke up, "Everyone loves Marietta. She is as good as she is lovely, and has the intelligence of a grown girl." The landowner realized that Maria's beauty needed no roses to enhance it.

By the time she was nine, Maria was sent to do the family marketing. She took time to be friendly, but returned home to help as soon as possible. Even in these brief contacts in town, the merchants recognized something special about this child sent to do a woman's chores. They often presented her with small gifts for which Maria thanked them warmly.

One day the grocer, Giocanni, gave her a nice red apple and a cookie. Enthusiastically, Maria thanked him and slipped the apple into her bag of groceries. Surprised, the grocer asked her what she was going to do with it. Maria replied cheerfully that she would give it to her brother Alessandrino as he was particularly fond of apples. Again, Maria thanked him warmly but made no move to eat the cookie. On being asked, she confessed almost apologetically that she wanted to take it as a treat to her little sister Ersilia. She thanked the grocer for being so good to her family and turned to go. Determined to do something for Maria, he handed her another cookie and said that this one must be for Maria herself. Not wishing to displease him, Maria ate the cookie there and thanked the grocer again.

Because of Maria's outstanding qualities — kindness, cheerfulness, obedience, and friendliness — many of the people in the area began to notice and comment on her. Maria was totally unaware of these comments, but her mother heard them. She would answer by saying, "She is only doing her duty," although from time to time she felt that Maria was truly a special child. Long after Maria's death, her mother was to state that she could never remember Maria voluntarily displeasing or disobeying her.

Financially, the Goretti family did not seem to prosper, even working in partnership with the Serenellis. Luigi, tired and rundown from overwork, fell a victim to the familiar multiple diseases of the marsh — typhus, malaria, meningitis, and pneumonia. During the ten days preceding his death, Assunta stayed by his bedside while ten-year-old Maria did all the cooking, ran the errands, and kept the children quiet. In addition, Maria prayed constantly. She often wore her Rosary around her wrist so it would be at hand in the odd moments she could find for its use. Before his death in May of 1900, Luigi begged Assunta to take the children and return to Corinaldo.

Luigi's death forced Assunta to take upon herself the man's job of laborer in the fields. She felt it would not be possible to move, so the family continued to live in the Pontine marshes. Maria assumed the position of "mother," doing the household chores necessary for the Goretti family and also for the Serenellis. Maria was not a good cook, but when rebuked for this fault she simply begged pardon for not being able to cook as well as her mother. Unfortunately, the family seemed to descend into even deeper poverty, largely due to the stinginess of Signor Serenelli. At one point, he locked up the cupboard to keep the children from using any food other than that which he allotted for meals. Assunta had to resort to going to the landlord in order to straighten out this problem, a move which served as one more count against her in the eyes of Serenelli.

One of the duties that Maria assumed at this time was that of teaching the children. She taught them their prayers and told them stories. Although she had had no formal education, Maria would come home from Church and repeat practically word-for-word the Bible stories she had learned there. Testimony from people who knew the family at this time contains many references to the fact that after her father's death, Maria accepted all her responsibilities and carried them out not only efficiently but with joy and cheerfulness. She never appeared tired.

When Maria played now, it was never to amuse herself, but only to please the younger children. A friend who brought a pot of soup as a gift for the family noted that Maria served all the others first and kept very little for herself. When questioned about this, Maria gave the excuse that her mother and older brother had to do heavy work and needed the nourishment, and the younger children were only babies and deserved the treat. In addition, Maria often comforted and cheered her mother, counseling total dependence on God and His Blessed Mother to provide and protect. The death of her father called forth reserves of strength from Maria.

Besides the loss of her father, the only other sadness which Maria mentioned was the long wait to receive First Communion. In Assunta's great respect for this sacrament, she told Maria that because of her inability to read, and because the family had no money for the proper clothes, she was afraid that Maria would have to wait. Maria's reply was, "You'll see, Mama; God will provide."

Maria herself thought of a person who would teach her Christian doctrine, and she promised to discharge all her household duties before walking into Conca to these lessons. Throughout the spring of 1902, eleven-year-old Maria seemed to grow spiritually as she prepared to receive her Lord. This love of God was translated into an even greater willingness to do her daily tasks lovingly for those around her.

In May, the local priest examined Maria and found her well prepared for the Sacrament. A white dress and lacy veil were not possible for Maria. Instead, on the morning of May 29, 1902, she arose and dressed in the gifts which the poor of the neighborhood had provided, gifts which the donors felt it a privilege to bring. Assunta had provided the dress, a wine-colored dress with tiny white dots. One friend had brought a pair of new shoes, another a veil, a third a candle. Another friend had woven a wreath of real flowers. At the last

minute, Assunta took the two treasures her husband had given her — a coral necklace and a pair of gold earrings — and put them on her child.

Maria's sensitive conscience led her to make one final preparation. She went around the house and begged pardon of her family members and the Serenellis for any wrong she might have done them.

This is the only known true photo of Maria. (She is on the left side, in the dark dress.) It was found in the 1980s among the effects of a woman in Maria's hometown.

Then the entire family began the walk to Conca for the ceremony.

The message the archpriest gave the first communicants was "purity at all costs." Maria was to show how well she had absorbed this lesson less than two months later.

During the month of June, Maria received Communion four more times. Also during this month, Alessandro Serenelli twice made advances to her. On both occasions he had managed to be alone with her in the house. This young man, nearly twenty, had been accepted by Maria as another brother. But suddenly, he was paying her compliments and attempting to come close and touch her. Instinctively, Maria recognized something of his intentions, and the purity of her soul was revolted. On both occasions he threatened to kill her if she mentioned the matter to anyone.

Maria did keep silent, but not through fear of harm to herself. Rather, she realized that exposing Alessandro would bring worry and grief to her mother and financial ruin to their family. During this month, she attempted to keep as far away from him as possible and to be in the company of her mother whenever Alessandro was near. She hoped by this to avoid any further occasions for confrontations.

It is interesting to note the factors that contributed to Alessandro's psychological make-up. The brutal murderer and would-be rapist was brought up by a stern and harsh father after the early death of his mother. During part of his teenage years he lived alone, doing work on the docks, and was exposed to all sorts of vices. He had some education, although his family lived most of the time in the same poverty as that of the Gorettis. Alessandro was quiet and fairly shy, and Assunta later testified that he kept the door to his room closed at all times. In his room he read all sorts of violent newspapers. Some biographers mention that he read a great deal of pornography, although in the strict sense this material was more sensational than sexually oriented, with news reports of brutality and murders. At any rate, it was unhealthy reading material.

On the other hand, from the time he and his father began living with the Goretti family, Alessandro exhibited many traits of goodness. He attended Mass and often joined in the saying of the family Rosary with the Gorettis. He was a hard worker in the fields, and from time to time actually defended one or the other of the Gorettis against the verbal abuses of his father.

By his own testimony, Alessandro first noticed how beautiful Maria was while praying the family Rosary. He also noticed that when praying, this girl really prayed, and did not simply mouth the words.

On Saturday morning, July 5, 1902, the Gorettis and the Serenellis were working in the field about one hundred thirty yards away from the house. After the noon meal, Signor Serenelli fell asleep under the stairs and the others returned to the field. Maria sat on the landing with her mending, watching over her sleeping baby sister. The other Goretti children were riding in the noisy threshing wagons with their mother.

Alessandro exchanged his place behind the lead oxen with Assunta and returned to the house. He brushed past Maria, went to his room, then came past her again carrying a handkerchief and went to the storeroom downstairs. It was later learned that he had sharpened and tapered a nine-and-a-half-inch pointed blade. He returned again to the house, and called Maria to come to him. When she called out to ask why, he repeated his demand. She told him she would not come unless she knew why she was needed. Alessandro came out to the landing and dragged her into the house. Any cry she made was drowned out by the steady hum of the thresher going round and round in the blazing sun. According to Alessandro, Maria's words were, "No! No! No! What are you doing? Do not touch me! It is a sin! You will go to hell!" Instinctively fighting to preserve her honor, Maria thought even at this traumatic time of the sin which would condemn Alessandro to hell. Although she fought with all her strength, she could hardly expect to hold out long against the husky young man. He pushed a handkerchief into her mouth to stifle her cries for help but, confronted with a will stronger than his own, he could not touch her.

At this point, Alessandro picked up the knife and began stabbing Maria. Reports as to the number of wounds vary, but fourteen major ones were treated at the hospital. Because of the threshing, those in the field did not hear Maria's cries for help. The baby on the landing awakened at the noise and began to cry, which awakened Alessandro's father at the foot of the stairs. Assunta then glanced up and noticed that the baby was unattended and in danger of falling off the landing. Signor Serenelli and Assunta ran toward the house, where they discovered Maria, who had begun to drag herself toward the door. When questioned, she answered in her direct way that Alessandro had stabbed her, saying "He wanted to make me do wrong and I would not."

The local doctor arrived, and as he was binding her wounds, Maria did not cry out with pain. From time to time, however, she said, "Oh, Alessandro, how unhappy you are! You will go to hell."

By the time the ambulance arrived, a crowd had gathered. Some men dragged Alessandro from his room, where he had shut himself up, and would have harmed him if the local police had not arrived and taken him away. Many of the others followed the ambulance, on foot, to the hospital.

During the trip to the hospital and the twenty hours of agony she spent before her death, Maria was conscious much of the time. She did not complain, and rarely even moaned with the pain. After asking twice for a drink of water (which was refused because her injuries were internal and water would have caused further damage), Maria gave up this comfort without complaint, as well as the comfort of having her mother beside her at night. The hospital had a rule that no visitors could stay overnight, and Assunta was forced to sleep in the back of the ambulance.

The priest was called soon after Maria's arrival at the hospital. Although the doctors performed surgery, none of the three doctors on the case had much hope for success. As the priest arrived, Dr. Bartoli assured him, "Father, you will have little to do. We are leaving a dying girl, but you are finding an angel."

The same priest who had given Maria her First Communion came to bring her the last. Before he gave her Viaticum, he asked her if she forgave her murderer with all her heart. Maria replied with no hesitation, "Yes, I do, for the love of Jesus, forgive him, and I want him to be with me in paradise . . . May God forgive him, because I already have forgiven him." Maria died shortly after three o'clock that afternoon.

Alessandro's trial began on Maria's birthday, October 16, 1902. In spite of the defense plea of insanity, Alessandro was found guilty. Because he was a minor, he received thirty years in prison instead of a life sentence. He was sent to a prison in Sicily where he spent the first eight years with no sign of remorse or regret for his crime. But one night, after living with a dead soul for all those years, Alessandro had a dream. He saw Maria in a field of flowers, holding out some white lilies to him. Within a few days after this dream, the local bishop

Painting of Maria, said by her mother to be the truest likeness of her

requested and obtained an interview with Alessandro. On November 10, 1910, Alessandro wrote a letter to the bishop begging God's pardon for the great sin he had committed.

Assunta took her children and returned to Corinaldo, in accordance with Luigi's last wishes. There she raised her family. She was able to obtain work as the housekeeper of the local priest, and worked there for many years.

Maria's heroic life and death were not forgotten. In 1929, the Passionist priests asked Assunta's permission to move Maria's body to the sanctuary of Our Lady of Grace. Pope Pius X had already held Maria up as an example of true devotion and an inspiration to youth.

In this same year, Alessandro was asked to give testimony in Maria's process for beatification. By this time, he had been released from prison and was living a quiet life as a laborer. Alessandro willingly gave his testimony, taking total blame, repeating that Maria's thoughts had been for his soul even at the moment of the attack, and relating the dream which had led to his conversion.

On Christmas Eve, 1937, Alessandro went to visit Assunta at the rectory to hear from her own lips the assurance of forgiveness. As he tearfully begged her pardon, she replied that she could hardly refuse when Maria had been so willing to extend this forgiveness. Assunta and Alessandro attended Midnight Mass together at Maria's shrine.

In 1947, Pope Pius XII beatified Maria. Because her death had been that of a martyr, no miracles were required for beatification. But thereafter, those in need began to cry to her for help, and such a shower of favors was received through her intercession that the two miracles necessary for canonization were speedily and unquestionably certified. Maria Goretti's canonization occurred on June 25, 1950, less than three years after her beatification.

Maria's own mother, by that time an old woman, was present, and the crowd was so huge that the ceremony had to be held outside, in front of Saint Peter's Basilica. The interval between Maria's beatification and canonization was one of the shortest of any cause recorded at the Vatican.

Alessandro lived out the rest of his life at the Capuchin monastery of Macerata. He became a Franciscan tertiary, and worked in the convent garden. He said, "The Brothers of Saint Francis, Capuchins from Marche, welcomed me with angelic charity into their monastery as a brother, not as a servant." He lived with the community until his death on May 6, 1970. In 1961, he wrote a letter as a spiritual testimony in which he said, in part, "I hope this letter that I wrote can teach others the happy lesson of avoiding evil and of always following the right path, like little children. I feel that religion with its precepts is not something we can live without, but rather it is the real comfort, the real strength in life and the only safe way in every circumstance, even the most painful ones of life." ✢

20

Maria Orsola Bussone
Italy, 1954-1970

Every Moment Is Important

"I go on thinking that God really wants us to be of service in bringing others to Him. . . . I have asked the Lord to put in my heart an immense desire to be His witness, that He would help me to choose Him totally," Maria Orsola Bussone wrote in a letter to a friend only a few months before her death. She had told her parish priest, "I am willing to sacrifice my life so that youth might understand how beautiful it is to love God!" Apparently God took her at her word. After her early death at the age of sixteen, her life and writings began to spread worldwide; her own words show how deeply this young, modern Italian girl had fallen in love with God.

Even on the day of her death she had begun to spread her message of love. A friend who was there that tragic evening, July 10, 1970, recalled "Notwithstanding all the human sorrow for her death, such a sensation of love and peace was created among us, down there at the seaside, that we had the certainty Mariolina had not left us, but she had gone forward to prepare a place for us and intercede for us."

Maria Orsola Bussone was born October 2, 1954, at Vallo Torinese, a small village near the Piedmont mountains. She grew up in a happy, harmonious family. Her father owned a factory near their home, and her mother was a skilled dressmaker. Her brother Giorgio, three years younger, completed the small and loving family.

Mariolina was baptized eight days after her birth in the parish church. She attended the Monasterolo nursery school where she is remembered for being helpful and prayerful, even as such a small child. She attended Primary School at Vallo. In this small school she was in a class of pupils of different ages, but she was bright and did well. She made her First Communion at seven and was confirmed at the age of eleven. After attending a Catholic middle school, she attended Galileo Ferraris, the Cirie State High School.

In 1967, at the age of twelve, Maria learned to play the guitar and, having a beautiful voice, she began to sing as a soloist in a small band with some young people of her parish. That same year, with her parents, she attended a Focolare Roman retreat. The retreat was the beginning of a revolution in Maria's thinking. She began a continuous self-questioning and comparison with her models Jesus and Mary. In her diary she writes about seeking happiness not in big things but in the small everyday things of life.

Maria at the microphone, singing with her group

In the summer of 1968, after taking part in a Focolare youth meeting, Maria wrote to Chiara Lubich, the founder of the Movement, "I want to thank you for these wonderful days and I want to tell you what I have understood. During these days I have understood that the key to our joy is the Cross. It is Jesus forsaken. I have made up my mind to choose God, to always love Him and especially when I am suffering... I want to become a tool in God's hands, following His wishes, and I want to do everything I can because it is the only thing worth living for, and I want all the young to learn what is true happiness and to love God."

In 1969, Maria won an essay contest, writing about the European Community, and was rewarded with a trip to Brussels, Luxembourg, and Strasburg along with eight other students. In another essay where she was asked to write about her favorite song, she says that she is drawn to songs which "offer something to the listener," not just those made to sell records. She says her favorite is a song called "I am looking for you," and that she likes it because it shows a need that young people feel today. She points out that many youth are always looking in vain for happiness, and points out, "Then, all of a sudden, after so much searching, we realize, to our great astonishment, but also with great joy, where God is; not far but very near us, in our neighbor, in the people we come across, in the sick, in the people who are disagreeable. In fact, Jesus has said that He is in all of us in this sentence: 'Anything you have done to the least, you have done to me.' After such a wonderful discovery, we too will then be able to say and sing: "I too am looking for You, and now I know where You are!'"

Maria was known as a happy, extroverted girl who was always willing to do something with or for others. She frequented the oratory at Vallo, a meeting place for the young, where she enjoyed the catechism classes, made friends, and enjoyed the social activities. She loved sports, especially swimming, cycling, skating, and skiing.

A normal adolescent, Maria occasionally developed crushes. One, in particular, was a boy named Sandro. Eventually, however, she made a definite choice: "I am ready to accept God's will; therefore it is Him I choose. So, good-bye Sandro! When I think of Sandro, though, I remember the 1968 meetings in Rome and so many things I enjoy. No, I have to choose God and that's it!"

A month later, she wrote in her diary, "I have understood that the only thing worth living, the only thing that makes me happy, is God. So I have decided to choose Him as a "whole" in my life, although the beginning has not been so positive. Anyway, I must live the present moment and I must not think about the past or the future."

The young Maria in a jaunty cap

Maria's letters to her friends show a maturity far above her age. In addition to the ability to analyze herself, she points out how when she fails she is ready to start again. She is also able to offer wise advice and spiritual guidance in an invitation to walk together to the goal of Christian love.

In one letter Maria writes, "Such is our life: it is a continuous starting again, it is a continuous picking ourselves up to take the path leading to God. It is very difficult, of course, to start all over again, but it is enough to have a little faith in God's love, which is in the love that God has for us. Even if we make mistakes, even if we have not loved God for days and days, even if we are cowardly mean creatures, God loves us in an extraordinary way, in fact, as water cannot help watering, as fire cannot help burning, so God cannot help loving and mostly when we have fallen."

In another, she reminds her friend, "At the end of our life, God will not ask us if we have been behaving like this or that person, if we had understood what we had been told about Him, but He will ask us if we have loved Him in our brothers and we shall have to answer for the talents He has given us and if we have made them work. Therefore, let us roll up our sleeves and start going ahead."

On April 5, 1969, Maria wrote to her friend Piero, "Last Sunday God made me understand one thing, but an essential one: that He alone, He alone is important, He is our only salvation, He is our joy, He is the freedom we young people seek and want but cannot find by just rebelling and doing whatever we like. We can only find it by doing His will. He has also made me understand another very impor-

tant thing, that everything, everything is love because He loves us with an immense love. What should we do, then? Since we want and yearn for love, we cannot turn down the greater, more sincere, more beautiful love that is offered us! We just have to dive head-first into such love."

Life was smiling on Maria Orsola and she was smiling back. Although she had made no firm decision, entries in her diary indicate she was thinking of her future. Her future, however, was not to be on this earth.

Maria as a young teen

In the summer of 1970, Maria had planned to spend part of her holidays at a summer camp at Cà Savio, near Venice, where she was going to be a group leader. She arrived there on July 3 along with her brother and forty children and teenagers from her own and two other parishes. By her bed at the camp, Maria hung a sign, a plan for her life, which read: "(1) See God in my fellow creatures. (2) Offer God to the others. (3) Follow God's will."

The evening of Friday, July 10, Maria had just come back from the beach where she had played her guitar and sung during the last meeting of the day and was getting ready for Mass. While she was drying her hair, a powerful electric shock from the faulty appliance struck her down. A few minutes later her cousin Marisa

Maria, photo taken in 1969

came to get her, and found her lying lifeless on the floor. Artificial breathing and heart massage were in vain.

Among the first to run to Maria Orsola was her brother Giorgio who, in front of his sister's lifeless body, reacted with deep faith, saying, "Maria is happy now, we have just to live the present moment."

Later, Giorgio gave this touching testimony: "What struck me most in my sister is the fact that every moment was important for her. I do not remember her doing great things, but every moment in her life belonged to God, and so it had to be lived to its fullness. Being joyful was typical of every day in Maria Orsola's life; even if sometimes she had a problem, she always tried not to show it, so that the people around her might be happy, and how many times I have been infected by her joy!"

Maria Orsola Bussone

Maria's body was brought to Vallo on Saturday night, and at about four in the morning on Sunday, Don Vincenzo said Mass at her home for her parents and the girls of the parish group.

The funeral took place on Monday and more than two thousand people attended. The cortège was led by the village band while a peal of bells resounded; the altar boys were dressed in red and the priest, wearing white robes, was surrounded by thirty fellow celebrants. There were also representatives of about fifty parish communities and many members of the Focolare Movement in the region. It seemed more of a celebration than a funeral.

Maria Orsola's mother gave Don Vincenzo the rough copies of many of her daughter's letters, together with other writings and her diary. Something of the secret this smiling girl kept in her heart, and which so many others had caught, was beginning to be seen. "Only now," said her father, "do we realize the reason for her serenity and for her joyful smile." And her mother added, "We have understood the depth of her soul only after her death."

The canonical process for Maria Orsola Bussone's beatification has been opened in her diocese. ✛

21

Mary Ann Long
United States, 1946–1959

Little Apostle of Consolation

"This is the way God wants me," the smiling young cancer patient told her visitor when the woman had asked why she didn't pray for a cure. With her lively and charming personality, Mary Ann Long made many friends, and her calm obedience to God's will for her impressed and inspired all who came in contact with her during her brief life on this earth.

At a very young age, Mary Ann Long suffered from all the tragic consequences of cancer, including pain and disfigurement, and in 1959 she lost her battle with the disease. How, then, is her life remembered not with grief but with joy, love, and thanksgiving? The answer to this question lies in the life of the child herself. Even at such a tender age, she had a definite mission in life, and she fulfilled this mission to the best of her abilities, bringing love, joy, and consolation to all who knew her.

———

Mary Ann was one of four children of a family from Kentucky. Misfortune had followed the family, leaving it in poor circumstances. Mary Ann's mother was ill and could not care for a sick child. At the age of three and a half, in spite of x-rays, radium, and the removal of her eye, Mary Ann was diagnosed as incurable at the tumor clinic in Louisville. The hospital could no longer keep her. The family doctor advised her parents to send her to Our Lady of Perpetual Help Home, which was run by the Dominican Sisters of Hawthorne, in Atlanta. The thought of sending their dying child so far from home and to strangers was terrible to her loving parents. However, no other option was financially possible, so they reluctantly agreed to let her go there until her mother could regain her health.

Sister Veronica, at that time superior of the home, saw Mrs. Long arrive in a taxi with the new patient. She was eager to meet this child about whom a social worker in Louisville had written to her: "This patient is a very loveable little girl and one who touches the hearts of all who come in contact with her."

As Sister walked out to greet the new arrivals, Mrs. Long felt apprehensive about Mary Ann's reaction to a woman who was dressed so strangely. Mary Ann had never seen a nun before. But before her mother's astonished eyes, she ran to the welcoming arms. Once inside, she was lovingly passed from one set of arms to another. Laughingly, she greeted each, sister and patient alike, with no shyness or hesitation.

One of the sisters described her first view of Mary Ann in this way: "She does look awfully tiny and kind of thin, but her face is round and happy-looking. One cheek is swelled badly, and the eye is closed. You should see her hair — it's so soft and curly." Mary Ann's one good eye was brown, and sparkled with the joy of life.

Mary Ann was distracted by the sisters while her mother sadly left. The sister on duty that night was afraid that Mary Ann would cry for homesickness. Instead, she slept quietly and in the morning investigated the entire ward. At the bed of one of the patients Mary Ann stopped, climbed up on the bed, sympathetically looked at the patient and stroked her hand. For the rest of her short life, Mary Ann was to continue to console all the residents of the home in her own cheerful and sympathetic way.

Tales of pious and religiously-oriented children are sometimes exaggerated, and sometimes the teller mistakes the innocence of childhood for something out of the ordinary. Mary Ann exhibited all the ordinary goodness of childhood, but there was also something special about her life and her ability to console those who came to console her.

Our Lady of Perpetual Help Home in Atlanta, Georgia, is a pleasant place of refuge and love for the poor who are suffering from incurable cancer. Although most of the residents are adults, child patients are not unknown there. The sisters who staff the home, the Dominican Sisters of Hawthorne, see more human misery and physical corruption in a single day than many others meet in a lifetime. These sisters truly understand what Christ meant when He said that those who serve the least of His brothers actually serve Him. They are able to see beyond the tragic outer shell of a patient to the presence of God in the soul within. Mary Ann's special gift was the ability to display her interior beauty despite her disfigured outer self. She strove completely to forget her own self in favor of the needs of others.

Mrs. Long had explained to the sisters that the family had no religious affiliations, and when asked if she wished Mary Ann to be baptized, she promised to consult with her husband and write her decision. The parents decided to ask the sisters to have Mary Ann baptized, and the patients joyfully prepared for the ceremony. A Methodist contributed a white satin nightgown she had received as a gift, and a Baptist patient made it into a white dress for the beginning of Mary Ann's Christian life.

The sisters tried to provide all the things possible to make a comfortable and happy home for their youngest patient. The other patients and friends of the home derived much pleasure from her childish joy in their small gifts. In addition to caring for her temporal needs, the sisters provided for Mary Ann's spiritual needs as well. She was intelligent and a quick learner, and the sisters taught her much about the love of God. When one of the sisters tried to explain the Stations of the Cross, she ended by lifting Mary Ann up close to the stations so she might see better. Sadly, Mary Ann said, "Oh, poor Jesus." This is perhaps a normal childish reaction to such a sad depiction. But Mary Ann seemed to take her lessons in religion and absorb them in a mature way for so young a child. Her prayer, "Jesus I love You with all my got," was as close as she could get to "with all my heart." She did not stop with the formal, rote prayers taught to her, but soon began adding her own intentions.

Once, Mary Ann wistfully questioned Sister Loretta about heaven, suggesting that it would be light and she would be able to see with both her eyes. "When I get to heaven," she said, "I'll have two good

Mary Ann was very proud of her membership
as a Brownie Scout

eyes and I'll run all around heaven and be able to see everybody there at once!"

Sister Loretta told her, "Heaven is everything that is perfect and is our true home, but this must not make us forget our work here, the things God put us here to do."

First Communion

The tiny four-year-old shocked Sister by her immediate grasp of this definition. Mary Ann said, "You mean we make it so bright and cheerful here that everyone will know what it'll be like in heaven?"

Mary Ann rarely cried, but when she did she usually had a good reason. Good reason or not, she would struggle against this display. One day when she was leaving the chapel with one of the sisters, the tears began to fall. When questioned as to the reason, she told the sister that she wanted to have Jesus come to her, as He came to everyone else. The sisters began to prepare her for First Communion, and promised to pray that she be allowed to make it within that next year.

Trying to explain to her what was meant by an examination of conscience, Sister Loretta doubted if she could grasp this concept. However, Mary Ann seems to have understood the "zamination," for after telling Sister of a particular piece of self-willed naughtiness she had performed that day, Mary Ann turned back to her prayers and with real contrition in her voice said "I'm sorry, Baby Jesus."

She was allowed to make her First Communion at the age of five, and was confirmed at six. She chose the name Joseph for her confirmation name, explaining that since he had taken care of Baby Jesus and Blessed Mother, he would also take care of her.

Mary Ann's parents loved her dearly. Financially they were unable to visit her often, but they came when they could. In spite of her cheerful behavior, her father was troubled at the thought of having sent his child to an "institution." When Mary Ann was six, her parents took her home with them, but after a short time her mother called the sisters and asked them to take her back. She said, "We just don't seem to be able to make her happy here."

Although Mary Ann loved her family, she was more comfortable at the home, away from the unkind stares of those outside her family who saw, at first, only her deformity. A few years later another attempt was made to take Mary Ann back to Kentucky. This, too, failed, and she spent the rest of her life with the sisters and patients she loved so dearly.

The retreat master of the nearby Trappist monastery paid a visit to Mary Ann soon after her first attempt to live at home. She told him about her family, her trip to Kentucky, and the bad children who had stared at her there. He asked her, "Mary Ann, do you want to help those children become good? They haven't been taught to be good and they need help." After Mary Ann indicated how willing she was to help, the priest explained to her how she could accept her disappointments, hide them, and offer them as a gift to the Baby Jesus to help these children. She never forgot the lesson, and if she ever shed tears after that, it was not over little things.

Some of Mary Ann's greatest joys came from the times her sister Sue was allowed to come and spend the summers with her. The two girls were very close, and Sue was the first of Mary Ann's family to follow her into the Catholic Faith.

Mary Ann had once asked a visiting priest if she might become a nun, and one of the sisters sewed little habits for Mary Ann and Sue to play in. After the girls were taken to a visit to a cloistered Visitation monastery, Sue began to slip off to the chapel when the two girls played at being nuns. Mary Ann continued to help the patients in the ward. One day, when Mary Ann could not locate Sue, she exclaimed in exasperation, "All I say is if all Sue wants to do is go to chapel and pray, she just better join another order. . . We work!" When the story was told at the sisters' recreation period, it naturally made the hard working Dominicans roar with laughter.

Mary Ann had a special gift for bringing laughter and joy to those at the home, no matter how serious or sad the occasion. Once, a Father Kerwick was hearing the confessions of the Catholic patients and came to Mary Ann's room. A few days before, Mary Ann had been given a little parakeet as a pet. "Just a minute, Father," she said. Going over to the parakeet's cage, she took it off the stand and left the room. She came back empty handed and explained, "Sister says parakeets repeat what you say, and I don't want him repeating my sins!"

Mary Ann loved to do things for other people. Often, her gentleness and cheerful acceptance of her own state in life made it easier for the other patients to accept their own problems. One patient was almost helpless. Mary Ann went often to help her brush her hair or do other small things the patient herself could not do. When Mary Ann asked this lady if she would like to say her night prayers with her, the lady admitted that she did not know how to pray. Mary Ann began to teach her and then enlisted the aid of others in the project. She was thrilled to become this patient's baptismal sponsor.

Mary Ann dressed as a little nurse; like any little girl she loved to play "dress up"

Another patient came to the home from Kentucky because her husband had deserted her after discovering she had incurable cancer. Mary Ann did not know the background of the case, but she recognized that the woman's spirit was crushed. She informed the lady that she, too, was from Kentucky. She brought the patient a drink of water, and became her special "nurse" in the next couple of days. This woman told one of the sisters, "Now I know why I came all the way from Kentucky. Years ago I was a Catholic. I've wanted to come back for a long time and didn't know how." That night she died. Again it seemed that Mary Ann had helped a soul to find God.

Mary Ann's mission appears to have been to live her own life in such acceptance of her state that she continually drew others to God. Her constant prayer was that her own family would become Catholic, and within a few years after her own First Communion, her three sisters, one by one, began to follow her example. The summer after

Mary Ann's death, her mother, too, was baptized, fulfilling one of Mary Ann's greatest wishes.

Mary Ann had often expressed a wish for a baby that she could care for. When Mary Ann was eleven, baby Stephanie came to live at the home. This tiny cancer victim was the seventh child of warm and loving parents. These parents, particularly the mother, found it very hard to give up their baby. Only the counsel of their priest had convinced them they should take Stephanie to the home.

Mary Ann met the parents at the door. Recognizing the parents' inner turmoil, she told them, "I didn't pray for a baby to be sick, but I prayed that if a baby was sick it would come here." Later, Stephanie's mother said that Mary Ann's words helped her to understand God's purpose for the baby. Her doctor and others had told her that the baby was useless, and the kindest thing would be simply to let it die. But Stephanie's mother understood the situation better after Mary Ann's remarks. In the mother's words, "Stephanie was needed; she wasn't useless; this child with a bandaged face and a heart full of love needed her. My whole attitude changed and as the months passed and we came back to see Stephanie the hurt healed and was replaced by a quiet joyful gratitude for her. Not only did she bring happiness to Mary Ann, but she brought it to all in the home."

Mary Ann, for her part, was an excellent nurse and a real help with Stephanie. She never complained when the baby kept her awake at night. She comforted Stephanie and helped to feed and care for her. Mary Ann seemed very pleased when Sister assured her that she really was a big help in caring for this child.

In September of 1958, Mary Ann's physical condition began to grow much worse. One of the sisters remembered that Mary Ann had always wanted to be a sister, and she was allowed to become a Dominican tertiary. When the sisters suggested that the ceremony be performed in her own room, Mary Ann insisted on going to the chapel, where she received the name of Sister Loretta Dorothy and the scapular of the Order of Saint Dominic.

A large growth appeared in Mary Ann's mouth, and it soon became impossible for her to eat normally. She never complained, and when her parents came for a visit and a sister suggested that they eat in the breakfast room rather than in her room as they had done on past visits, Mary Ann was quick to understand the suggestion. "Oh yes,

Sister, because it wouldn't be good for Mama and Daddy to watch me struggling to eat." Even in this small matter, Mary Ann was concerned about her parents rather than about herself.

Shortly before this visit, Mary Ann had been thrilled to hear that she had merited the highest award of Catholic Girl Scouts, the Marian Award. Normally, the award is presented at the cathedral, but the bishop sent a young priest to perform the ceremony at the home. Her Girl Scout troop

Mary Ann dressed as a Hawthorne Dominican novice

and many of her friends were present. When a wheelchair was brought to her room, she pleaded to be allowed to walk down for the ceremony, and could be dissuaded only when the doctor pointed out that she might pass out before receiving the award. When the qualifying questions were asked, she answered in a weak but clear voice, and the priest was so visibly touched that his voice cracked several times during the ceremony. Afterwards the troop members congratulated her and presented her with a little stuffed dachshund which they had autographed. Mary Ann was exhausted but begged to be allowed to keep her uniform on until her parents arrived that night. She rested on a lounge chair for the long wait and when she finally heard the elevator, she summoned all her strength to stand up and walk to the door of her room. She stood at attention, wearing the medal, and proudly gave her parents the Girl Scout salute. When a sister brought in Cokes for all of them, Mary Ann realized she could not drink it. Not wanting to spoil her parent's short visit, she didn't tell them, just quietly held her glass and then set it aside unobtrusively.

Shortly before Christmas, another serious hemorrhage occurred. The sisters lit the candle which now always stood ready at Mary Ann's bedside. Mary Ann held it and over and over she repeated, "Dear Jesus, I love You."

In January, Mary Ann was visited by a self-styled faith healer. This boy's mother had at one time been a patient in the home. As he entered her room, he greeted her with the words, "The Lord Jesus can heal you, Mary Ann." When she made no reply, he repeated his statement.

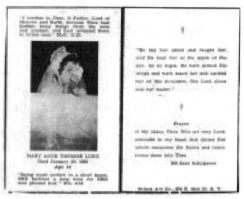

Mary Ann's memorial card

Mary Ann looked at him. "I know Jesus can heal me," she said. "I know He can do anything. It doesn't make a bit of difference whether He heals me or not. That's His business."

Mary Ann died quietly in her sleep during the night of January 18, 1959. In her hands she clutched her Rosary, which she had been praying when she fell asleep.

At Mary Ann's funeral, Bishop Hyland said, "From the viewpoint of the world, the death of Mary Ann was indescribably sad. This viewpoint fails to take into account that the primary purpose of our existence on earth is to know, love, and serve God, and to prove thereby our worthiness of eternal happiness with Him in heaven."

None who knew her can doubt that Mary Ann, in the space of the twelve years allotted to her, did indeed know, love, and serve her God, both with fidelity and joy. ✢

22

Montserrat Grases Garcia

Spain, 1941-1959

Instrument of Happiness for Others

"We're the happiest family in Barcelona," Montserrat Grases told her father. When I die, I don't want anyone to be sad. There has to be joy."

Montserrat Grases

The Spanish teenager knew she was dying from deadly bone cancer, but instead of thinking of herself, she constantly strove to console her family and friends. She frequently said, "I assure you that from heaven I'll help you a lot. I'll never leave you."

The life of Montserrat Grases is an inspiration for those who, in any walk of life, try to give their existence a higher meaning. Through the everyday things of life, Montserrat became a holocaust of love for God and an instrument to make others happy. The life of this young Spanish girl proves that sanctity isn't something removed from ordinary life; sanctity lies in serene, cheerful, simple, and yet heroic correspondence to the will of God. Montse, as her friends called her, died when she was only 17 years old.

Her brief years, lived with love and simplicity, and united to suffering, show that the way to true happiness has God as its beginning and its end. Her cause for beatification has been entered in Rome.

Montse's life is detailed in *Faces of Holiness*. ✢

23

Santos Franco Sánchez
Spain, 1942-1954

Small, But Large in Faith

"Help me because I am so small . . . Mother, how I love you." The little boy, wracked with pain, spoke softly. His mother crossed to the bed and asked if he were speaking to her. Santos clarified: "I am talking to my Blessed Mother, who is right here."

Santos as a student at the Carmelite minor seminary

"God's will be done," whispered the little boy. At the age of only eleven years, Santos Franco Sánchez had learned and lived a simple faith so well that today he is being considered for the honors of the altar. At the height of his intense suffering from the deadly meningitis which killed him, this young child spoke to his family, gathered at his bedside. "Soon I am going to heaven; I have very little time left. I will not forget you. I love you very much. Don't cry, because I am happy. What do sufferings matter? Heaven! How beautiful; God and the Blessed Mother are there."

In most respects, Santos Franco Sánchez was a normal child. He was playful, sometimes mischievous, tranquil but not quiet, and he spent most of his short life playing and enjoying himself with friends and family. As a schoolboy, he had aspirations to grow up and enter the Carmelites. At a tender age, however, he was called by God to become a holocaust of pain. Although small in stature, it was with the maturity of a giant in faith that he responded, "Thy will be done."

His story is found in *Faces of Holiness*. ✛

24

Sonia Diaz Parga
Spain, 1970-1987

A Girl Who Ascended Rapidly

The day of her First Communion, little Sonia Diaz seemed like the living dead. She wouldn't talk, and her mother and sister tried everything to make her smile for her photograph, but nothing worked. All day she seemed sad and serious. At last, that evening, in the intimacy of her own home, she finally explained to her mother, "Mama, I am sad because Jesus didn't tell me anything — nothing, nothing, nothing! — when I received Him in Communion." Somehow, she had gotten the idea that Our Lord was coming to talk to her, and she felt deceived.

Sonia Diaz Parga

It wasn't until Sonia was a teenager that Our Lord spoke deep in the soul of this Spanish girl. Without the need for words, she understood His love. Hers was one of those souls, small but mature in love, that God has given to our world because He reveals Himself clearly to the small and humble and confounds the wise. In the last year of her life, she was much happier than ever before. She was on fire with the love of Jesus, and that love filled her life.

Sonia was born October 2, 1970, in Monforte de Lemos, a small town in the province of Lugo, Galicia region, in the northwest part of Spain. When Sonia was a year and a half old and her sister Maria was nearly six, the family moved to Barcelona. Her father left the family, and then she, her mother Isura, and her sister moved in with Isura's mother. Isura determined to bring her girls up, with the help of her mother, as good Christians. She wanted them to have a totally Catholic education. When it was time for Sonia to begin school, her mother enrolled her at the school of the Sisters of Charity of Saint Vincent de Paul.

As a young child, Sonia had a strong and stubborn character, but finally she learned that when her mother said something, neither tears nor temper would change her mind. Daily, her mother prayed that the Holy Virgin would help her with the education of her daughters, and she is convinced that the Virgin heard her prayers.

From the time she was very young, Sonia and her sister attended catechism classes at their parish church of Our Lady of Nuria. Even after making First Communion, they continued attending the classes because their mother believed they were important for their formation. Sonia internalized many of the lessons she learned here and displayed a particular affection for the souls in purgatory. She had a lot of earaches because of bad teeth when she was young. Her mother didn't know anything about this until one day Sonia burned herself and her mother noticed blisters on her leg. She asked the child, "Sonia, isn't that painful?"

Sonia replied, "For sure it hurts!"

Isura then asked her, "Then why didn't you complain or say anything?"

Sweetly, the child responded, "Because I offered it up for the souls in purgatory so they would suffer a little less."

Maria says that Sonia was a normal child, a prankster like many children her age, and very alert and intelligent. Sonia was charmed by sweets, and sometimes if the girls were given bonbons, Sonia would propose that they save some of them for later. However, her greed was stronger than her intent, and she would eat her own and then also eat her sister's candy.

Sonia had a special gift of telling jokes, and she could spend hours telling them without ever getting tired. Her sister Maria says that her friends used to say that when Sonia was older she was going to make a large amount of conquests.

Between the ages of thirteen and fourteen, Sonia passed through a crisis of faith. During this time, when Isura and Sonia discussed matters of faith, sometimes Sonia left her mother speechless and worried that in time her daughter might become irreligious. Fortunately, the crisis didn't last long, although it left Sonia somewhat cold about her faith. At fourteen, she began studying at the School Vedruna de Grace and attended the church of the Virgin of Grace.

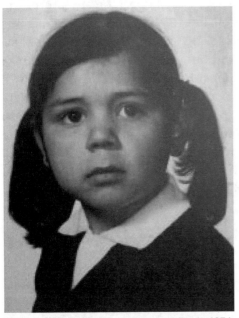

School picture of Sonia at the age of five in 1974

By this time, Sonia had become a vivacious and somewhat worldly girl. She wanted to dress in the latest fashions, wearing brand names when possible. In the summer, when the family went to Galicia on vacations, she wanted to attend all the parties. She liked television so much that she watched it as much as she could and didn't like anyone to interrupt her. She even got up early to watch favorite programs.

At sixteen, Sonia had finished grammar school and started the first level of secondary education, which in Spain is called BUP (*Bachillerato Unificado Polivalente*). On March 30, 1985, she went for the first time to the shrine of Our Lady of Can Cerda outside Barcelona, a former place of apparitions of Our Lady and presently a sanctuary of Marian devotion. Later, she wrote to the Augustines at Alicante that she believed her conversion began from this time. Sonia wrote, "On this day my mother secretly consecrated me to the Virgin and asked her to take me under her protection, and thanks to God the Virgin heard my mother's words. At that time I had become cold in my faith and didn't want to go to church and had stopped going to catechism. From this time, though, God was working in the innermost part of my soul."

"This same day my mother and I had a chat, and we came to a compromise. I wouldn't make the spiritual exercises she wanted me to make, but each day I would recite the Rosary instead."

"Some months passed and I had just completed the first year of BUP and was just about to go on vacation before the second year. I had always gotten good marks because I was responsible in my school work. But after the first evaluation, I was missing 4 assignments and was suspended. This was a strong blow for me and I thought, 'If I study and still am suspended, what hope is there for my future?' So I took no rest and worked. I got up early. All I thought about was studying. Finally came the week of the exams of the second evaluation, and I didn't feel secure. And one day, half an hour before taking one of the most difficult exams, I made a promise. I told Jesus, 'Look, if You will help me I promise I will make the spiritual exercises.' In other words, I offered what cost me the most. I was able to make up all the suspended assignments. My friends congratulated me on seeing such a big change in my work and my grades, and the professors told me that this was what I should make. I was happy with what had happened, and regretfully I decided to keep my promise and make some days of retreat."

"Casually, my mother told me that to keep my promise we would make four days of retreat during Holy Week in a church of Alicante."

At first, Sonia protested, telling her mother that she had only promised a short retreat at the end of the week. Her mother prevailed by intriguing Sonia with the idea of getting out of Barcelona and going to Alicante and learning about another city. Finally, Sonia decided that it was a reasonable idea and that she could fulfill her promise to Jesus and have a clear conscience.

First Communion, 1978

Sonia, her mother, two other ladies, and her friends Maria Antonia and Maria José went to Alicante to celebrate Holy Week with Father Manuel Navarro. Father Navarro was too busy to preach the spiritual exercises of Saint Ignatius, but he dedicated several talks to the

Barcelona people, and all of them followed the Holy Week services very devotedly.

"In that Holy Week, I didn't die with Jesus; however I learned many things from my mother about the significance of the ceremonies. Jesus didn't give me the gift to understand. And here, as I said, since I didn't die with him I didn't have the right to come back to life with him, but he gave me that right with his infinite mercy. That Easter Sunday, Father Navarro invoked the Holy Spirit on those of us from Barcelona. That night, before we left the city, in front of the

The last photo of Sonia, two days before she died

tabernacle of Saint Isabel church, without knowing why, I began to cry, and to cry with a true grief, and my tears transformed into a great interior happiness. And now I want to note a detail. It was March 30, 1986, exactly one year after my mother made the secret consecration of me to the Virgin of Can Cerda. After this I began to go to daily Mass and to spend an hour of adoration in front of the Blessed Sacrament. I don't know why; I only know that here I met Jesus with pleasure."

"In the next month and a half I was discovering, next to Jesus in the Blessed Sacrament, many things. I remembered that I wanted to be the most what he wanted me to be. If you want me to marry, I will marry. If you want me to remain single, I will stay single. If you want me as a nun, then I will be a nun. I will be the best nun of all, if you want it too."

Sonia went to talk to Father Navarro on May 14. The priest made a slight suggestion to Sonia that she might have a vocation to religious life. Sonia wrote, "While talking to him at a certain moment I thought that no, I didn't have one. But only a second later, I felt such a deep peace that it seemed to me a marvelous thing. When I recall that moment, I tell myself it was as if I had spent all my life waiting for someone to come and tell this to me."

A change came about in Sonia. A change that was an ascension, step-by-step, into intimacy with the merciful heart of Christ. One day, she joyfully told her mother, "Oh, Mama, how lucky we are to have the love of God! Before, there was a vacancy inside of me. I saw a fashionable sweater on a friend and I thought if I could have this sweater I would be happy. Or other things. Then I would get them and be happy and content for only a day or two. But now that I have God, I am full of happiness. I don't need anything else!"

Sonia used all her time wisely, especially for mental prayer. That was one of the constants of her new life. When she was on the bus or in a car, she read the magazine *Ave Maria* or a religious book, and her reading helped her in her ascent. When she was at home, if her mother was doing something and didn't need her help, Sonia would read aloud to her mother. One day, her mother told her, "Sonia, I can't meditate and I can't pray like you. Can you help me and tell me how?"

Sonia's response was, "No, Mama, don't worry about this. Go to the sanctuary and ask Jesus. He will show you how, little by little."

She practiced mortification with delicate and heroic strength. She began to give up many things. The television was the first thing she cut off. Gradually, she also gave up the fashionable clothes and preferred to wear modest blouses and skirts.

Sonia was always willing to help those who needed it. One day her sister left her with the children, and when the time for the last Mass came, it seemed as if she wouldn't be able to go. She was preoccupied about this until she stopped and thought. Then she said to herself, "How silly of me. If Jesus wants me to go, he will arrange it." Then she returned to her usual tranquil self. A little later, there was a knock on the door. It was her friend Paloma, from the Centro Torxa of Opus Dei. Quickly, Sonia said, "Paloma, you have arrived like rain from heaven. Please stay with the children while I go to Mass." Then she ran to Jesus in the Eucharist.

On returning to Alicante, she joined the Union Seglar Association (Lay Union Association) to help her on the road she had started. She made the spiritual exercises in the house of *Mater Salvatoris* (Mother of the Savior), located on the top of Tibidabo Mountain, which crowns the city of Barcelona, with the youth of this group in September, 1986. She left here full of happiness and with many good ideas. Many of the things they talked about inspired meditation, which she wrote

On a skiing trip in 1987

in the form of her thoughts. She was only sixteen, but her soul had begun to experience a supernatural life.

On May 26, 1987, Sonia was confirmed at the cathedral of Barcelona, along with other students of the *Union Seglar*. Her intense piety began to set her apart from the others. In addition to her studies, she always made time to visit the sick and poor. It was as if Our Lord was preparing her to receive the gift of going to heaven. Many people have testified that they saw her often absorbed in prayer.

Father Navarro remembers that one day he had planned a trip to a crystal factory as an outing for the youth. When he invited Sonia, she asked him if Jesus had been there. When he told her no, she said, "Then I am not going. I am not interested. I prefer to be here in prayer."

On Saturday, July 25, Sonia went to the mountain shrine at Montserrat with her friend Maria Antonia. They wanted to visit the virgin of Montserrat and gain the special indulgences of the Marian jubilee. On their return to Barcelona, Sonia told Maria Antonia, "How good it would be if this same day we could go to heaven — we would enter so clean!" Perhaps she had a presentiment that she was coming to the end of her life.

Sonia died in a car accident on the way to Zaragoza three days later, July 28, 1987. It was planned as a jubilee trip to the Virgin of Pilar. Sonia wanted to give special thanks to the Virgin for her religious vocation, and because her mother had given her permission to enter the monastery of the Augustines in Alicante.

The group left Barcelona in two cars. Father Navarro was in the front seat of one, and a seminarian was driving. Sonia was sitting in the back between her friends Antonia and Maria José de los Santos. Near the town of Fraga, when the group was almost finished saying the Rosary, they had a flat tire and the car flipped over. Only Sonia was seriously hurt. She received a hard blow on the head and began to bleed abundantly. She was taken from the car and Father Navarro gave her the sacraments. She was taken first to the hospital of Lerida and then, by helicopter, to a large hospital in Barcelona.

Sonia's mother, sister, and a religious aunt came quickly to the hospital. Sonia gave a last good-bye to her mother, more with her face and her heart than with her lips. At eleven that night, her soul flew to be with the One who was her desire from the time of her conversion.

Sonia was buried on July 31 in the cemetery of Cerdanyola. Sonia had always been proud that she was born on the day devoted to the guardian angels, and she had a great faith in and devotion to her own guardian angel. An angel is sculpted on her niche to guard her resting place with devotion. The stonemason also put her photo and one of her sayings on the niche: "I want to go to heaven because I see that it is the will of God. There I can love like I wasn't able to love here, and I will be able to make others love Him." ✛

25

Stephen Kaszap
Hungary, 1916–1935

Boy Scout, Athlete, and Jesuit Novice

As the nurse and the priest entered the room where the dying young man lay, they realized he was no longer conscious. His open eyes were fixed on the crucifix and Marian medal in his hands, but he did not see the visitors. They found his final message, scrawled on a paper on the patient's bedside table: "God be with you! We will meet in heaven! Do not weep, this is my birthday in heaven. God bless you all!"

The priest anointed him and gave him absolution and the papal blessing. Then Stephen Kaszap stopped breathing, and his soul slipped quietly away.

Only a few weeks before, Stephen had written in his journal, "Finally! Eureka! I found what I have for so long searched for, but could not find. What is it? It is grace, the grace to recognize God's gifts always, and never to resist it but to follow it and trust in it, so that it can mold our souls."

Servant of God Stephen Kaszap

If, that day, he had only just realized the grace he writes of, it had nonetheless worked, hidden in the soul of this young Hungarian, for many years. He had offered "my whole life as a sacrifice to the Sacred Heart of Jesus for my own and other people's many horrible sins." Although Stephen Kaszap had planned to spend this life as a Jesuit priest, his offering was accepted, and God took him to Himself before the age of twenty.

———

Stephen was born March 25, 1916, in a small town near Budapest, Hungary. His father was chief supervisor at the local post office and his mother was a devoted homemaker. Stephen was the third of five children of this devout and affectionate Catholic couple.

As a young child, Stephen was happy and loving, although he sometimes displayed obstinate, aggressive behavior and, when teased by his brothers, was known for sudden fits of temper when he would fly into a blind fury and throw whatever he could grab with his small hands. He was always willing to help with the daily chores and loved to whistle while he worked. Stephen received his first Holy Communion on May 21, 1925, at the age of nine.

At thirteen, Stephen was sent to a boarding school conducted by Cistercian monks. An early riser, Stephen formed the habit of regular prayer and served Mass whenever possible. He wasn't, however, above the usual schoolboy mischief. As he himself said, "I have no doubt at all that I often irritated and annoyed the teachers. It seems to me now that the years at the *Lycée* just flew past. Hard work for exams, very pleasant vacations, and wonderful excursions with my fellow students are what I remember best about my student days."

At the *Lycée*, Stephen began to write a daily journal, a practice he continued until his death. In it, we can begin to see some of the secrets of his soul.

In 1931, his junior year, Stephen joined a sodality known as the Congregation of Mary. The purpose of the group was to increase the members' devotion and love of Our Lady and to spread this devotion to their fellow students by word and example. The group met twice a month in a small chapel of their own beside the great nave of the college church. Stephen joined in all the activities of the group enthusiastically, and at one time served as its secretary.

Throughout his school years, Stephen was an active member of the Boy Scouts. He felt that "the boy scout, par excellence, should be an example in everything. He is never rude nor silly, but earnest and manly; at the same time, he is always joyful." Apparently, Stephen fit his own model of the good scout. A former patrol leader says of him: "Whatever I asked, he carried out without argument or excuse. I could always trust him completely and always count on his support."

The same man remembers when Stephen was elected assistant patrol leader: "One day after Steve had been elected, he was assigned to practice his duties as assistant patrol leader. This involved giving commands in a loud voice to the troop drawn up in military formation. Obviously excited, Steve's voice faltered and the troop began to laugh. Steve's pride was really hurt."

Apparently he overcame that incident and was always in the center of all the scouting activities. He became proficient at bookbinding, won many of the memory games the troop played, and carried out all his assigned tasks at camp with no grumbling word of protest. Later, he became a patrol leader and his journal is filled with descriptions of the annual summer camping trips. A fellow scout said, "Steve often left the camp to go for walks in the forest. He loved nature because he understood its language." His patrol leader testified that "Steve got up every morning earlier than the others to go to the edge of the forest to pray." He always attended the morning Mass before returning to the activities of the day.

Steve loved bicycle trips and took many of them. After his eleventh-grade year, he earned some money as a tutor and, putting it together with other funds, was finally able to buy a bicycle of his own. That year he took a bike trip and on the way attended the Boy Scouts' international jamboree at Godollo.

Stephen was an active Boy Scout

During his school years, Stephen was fortunate to have an excellent gymnastics teacher and he became an outstanding athlete, winning a number of medals. In 1934, at one tournament he won gold medals on the combined bars and the high bars, as well as in horse racing. He was junior champion of his school district, and happy to win the honors for his school in the regional games.

Stephen as a young novice

In the ninth grade, Stephen became interested in a variety of intellectual pursuits, and his journal grew much larger. In addition to his thoughts and the record of his daily events, he began to write quotations, poetry, formulae, and various other things. His interests widened so much that he began to do poorly in his schoolwork. By the end of the tenth grade, his school marks had slipped so much that it shocked him back to better habits of concentration. He poured all his effort into doing better and was able to graduate from twelfth grade with a straight-A average. He wrote, "It was God's voice that guided me in my studies and helped me to carry them out with dedication." By this time, Stephen had chosen to follow a call to a religious vocation and to give his life to God.

Stephen entered the Jesuit novitiate, Manressa, in July of 1934 at the age of eighteen. Something about him made him stand out from the other novices. He reflected an inner maturity and displayed a warm, calm, reserved nature while at the same time being informal and friendly. He was well liked by both his teachers and his peers. He set his sights toward growing in the spiritual life and the practice of virtues. He aimed for higher ground, but he did this with good sense. "Sanctity does not consist of being faultless, but rather in not compromising with my weaknesses. Do I resign myself to them? If I fall a hundred times, I get up a hundred times and continue to fight resolutely."

Moral virtue was not easy for Stephen; he had to fight to control his instincts and passions. He confessed to his novice master, "My youth was pure but I was quite agitated as a teenager. I am only sorry that I was not able to go to Holy Communion much earlier in my life." In his journal, he writes more than once of having to fight temptations. He fought these battles as he had all others, with the strength and will of a champion.

Stephen loved and respected the saints. He took notes about their lives and talked about them to others. And of the Queen of Saints he wrote, "Love your Heavenly Mom! You love and long for your mother very much but, look, you'll find an even holier mother in the Virgin Mother! Love her and trust her unconditionally."

When Stephen entered the novitiate, he appeared to be in excellent health, although the physical exam showed an elevated fever which the doctor attributed to nerves. His heart was full of joy. The very next day, however, he became hoarse and soon lost his voice. When his voice returned, his tonsils needed attention. At Christmas, his ankles became swollen and he could barely walk due to arthritic pains. Pus-filled abscesses appeared on his fingers, neck, and face, and he became bedridden with tonsillitis. Stephen went through these trials with a sunny heart and wrote, "Any cross God gives must be car-

Stephen, fourth from the right, with his fellow athletes

ried with joy. A little illness is more useful than ten or twenty years spent in health." He suffered a near-fatal nosebleed, high fever, and pleurisy.

Accepting God's will, on March 2, 1935, Stephen wrote, "I suffer gladly for Christ and I don't run from pain." He got better, but then his fever went up again and he was taken to the hospital. Surgery was scheduled for March 19, the feast of Saint Joseph. Stephen whispered to his novice master, "I trust in Saint Joseph very much. How small our sufferings are and how much the Church needs them! These thoughts make suffering much easier for me." During Stephen's recuperation in the hospital, he began to help and influence the other patients. He returned to Manressa, but began to suffer from sores and

abscesses again. It soon became obvious that he did not have the required health to continue in the novitiate, and the superiors decided to send him home, telling him that they would welcome him back when his health improved.

On October 18, 1935, Stephen wrote, "Sacred Heart of Jesus, grant that I might empty myself com-

A good gymnast, Stephen displays his form

pletely! I do not want to reserve anything for myself, for my own intentions, not even my prayers, my sufferings, or anything else. Everything is yours, you gave them to me and I give them back to you, Sacred Heart. I want to serve the Seat of Love, Your Most Sacred Heart, with love and suffering."

The day of leaving the novitiate was the saddest of Stephen's entire life. His colleagues gathered in the common room where he bade each of them farewell. Stephen left with a heavy heart, but accepting everything as God's will, saying, "My whole life should be a continuous 'Yes' to God."

Stephen went home in early November, and by the 8th he was admitted to the hospital again. The diagnosis was erysipelas, so he spent two weeks in the hospital for contagious diseases. In December,

Stephen in the novitiate

his tonsils were removed. After ten days, he was allowed to go home. Before he left, he spent two hours playing with a nephew who had had ear surgery and was in the same hospital.

Stephen went home on December 14. Before nightfall, he was shaking with chills, and his fever rose. On the morning of the 15th he could no longer speak. On December 16, the doctor diagnosed a tumor in his throat and he was admitted to the hospital again. His mother spoke to the chaplain and then told her son farewell; she did not realize it was the last time she would see him alive.

An emergency tracheotomy was performed at about three in the morning. As soon as Stephen regained consciousness, he wrote a note requesting a priest, but the nurse ignored it, convinced that his life was in no danger. At five, the night nurse was relieved. As the day nurse bathed his sweat-soaked face, Stephen wrote a note indicating he would like the last rites. The nurse went at once to fetch the priest. At ten minutes past six, God's young athlete raced home. ✢

26

Saint Teresa of Jesus Fernández Solar
Chile, 1900-1920

The Fourth Teresa

"I am the happiest person on earth. I desire nothing more because my entire being has been seized by God, who is love."

Saint Teresa of Jesus of the Andes, as she came to be known, was a young contemplative nun whose entire spirituality was marked with joy. The first canonized saint of Chile, she is also the fourth saint of the Carmelite order to bear the name Teresa.

This young Chilean girl discerned her path of personal sanctity, set her feet sturdily on the way, and walked swiftly and surely to holiness. She died in 1920 at the age of 19, after only one year in the religious life. Less than a lifetime later, we are already permitted to hold her life as an example of heroic fidelity to the will of God and a beacon of Christian joy.

Sister Teresa in her Carmelite habit

Little-known outside her own country, Saint Teresa set forth a simple way to holiness that everyone can follow. Just as the "little way" of Saint Thérèse of Lisieux rapidly spread from Europe throughout the world, today the perfume of this new flower of the Americas is beginning to spread her message from our own corner of the world.

The story of Saint Teresa of Jesus of the Andes is detailed in *Faces of Holiness.* ✢

27

Venerable Teresita González Quevedo, Ca.Ch.
Spain, 1930–1950

The Virgin's Mirror

December 13, 1944, was an exciting day for a number of the students at the Carmelite Sisters of Charity's high school on the Plaza de San Francisco in Madrid. Recently, a sodality of Our Lady had been formed, and the girls were to make their consecration and choose their motto that day. Thirteen-year-old Teresita Quevado wrote out her chosen motto in which she had expressed an immense aspiration: "Mother, may those who see me, see you." The motto was etched on her medal of the sodality.

Venerable Teresita González Quevedo

Baptized with the long name Maria Teresa Josephina Justina González Quevedo y Cadarso, she had always been called Teresita, but she lived the Maria of her name. She had a special fondness for the Blessed Virgin from her earliest days, but in her own words, "Since I have become a sodalist, I love the Blessed Virgin infinitely more than before." Teresita kept this love for the Virgin, trying hard each day to mirror her virtues for love of Jesus, until the final moments of her life. Her last words were, "How beautiful, O Mary, how beautiful you are!"

Explaining her Marian devotion to her cousin, Teresita said, "I love Our Lord with all my heart. But He wants me to love Our Lady in a special way and to go to Him with my hand in Mary's." Years later, her uncle, a Jesuit priest, asked her, "How did you begin to have such love for the Blessed Virgin?" She replied, "The Virgin herself gave me this devotion. Since childhood, when Papa would take us into his room to make the daily offering with him, I delighted in the prayer, "Oh, my Queen and my Mother, I give myself completely to you."

———

Teresita was born on April 14, 1930, the third child of the prominent physician, Dr. Calixto Quevedo, and his wife. She was born in Madrid, only a year before the fall of the Spanish monarchy.

Teresita's mother described her children in a letter to her sister-in-law when her youngest was three: "Louis has the manner of an army general, Conchita is quiet and thoughtful. . . Teresita is a bundle of happiness. Everyone loves her. . . pretty as a picture, but terribly self-willed. Perhaps we have indulged her more than we should

because she is the youngest. Whatever the reason, she cannot be crossed. We shall have to do something about it."

"*No me gusta!*" (I don't like it!) was Teresita's frequent comment at the table. Her finicky appetite often led to such outbursts of rudeness. She later said, "After such disagreeable outbursts — there were a number of them before I received my First Holy Communion — Tia (Teresita's aunt) would watch for the first sign of sorrow in my face. I never apologized, I am ashamed to say. What patience and kindness she possessed! Not a word about my bad behavior to me, nor to Mama and Papa. She taught me many lessons in that way — patience and repentance. Without a word, she forced me to grow truly ashamed of myself."

Teresita at three years

The happy but headstrong little girl apparently took the matter of her self-control upon herself. After her First Communion, her father noticed quite a change in Teresita. He wrote to his brother, "The extraordinary power she had acquired over her quick, impulsive nature touched me deeply."

Later, as we learn from her confessor and her notes, she found another aid to self-control; this was her love for Mary. Every time Teresita triumphed over her revulsion for certain foods, or managed to put away her own will, she silently counted the incident as a little gift for Mary.

During much of the time of the Civil War in Spain, the Quevedo family lived away from their apartment in Madrid. During one of their stays in a fishing town, the cook noticed cakes and breads disappearing from the larder. Teresita's sister later confessed that Teresita had "snitched" them to take to the children of the fishermen. Even the plainest of fare from the wealthy Quevedo household was a rare treat for these children.

After the war, the family moved back to Madrid, where the girls attended Our Lady of Mount Carmel Academy. Teresita worked hard and made relatively good grades, but she also got into her share of schoolgirl mischief. At a designated period each day, the students were all supposed to be working in absolute silence on handwork. On one occasion, Teresita was embroidering a large tablecloth and enjoying a forbidden conversation with her cousin, Angelines. Suddenly the two magpies heard the measured tread of a sister coming down the hall. Angelines had no book or embroidery; what was she to do? Quickly, Teresita threw the large tablecloth over Angelines, and with a smile and a nod Sister passed by the industriously sewing Teresita.

Teresita at her First Communion

Each year, the academy girls of a certain age made a retreat. In 1941, at the age of eleven, Teresita would normally have been too young to attend. However, she asked for and received special permission to go along with the other girls. During the retreat, each girl kept a little notebook of points to remember from the lectures and discussions. It is probable that Teresita did not understand all the items in the discussions, but one thought which the priest presented, and which Teresita quickly grasped, was the necessity of making a resolution for life. Teresita's resolution, later found in this notebook, was: "I have decided to become a saint."

The road Teresita decided to travel to fulfill this resolution was paved with numerous small conquests of her own will. Always, her companion and guide on this road was Our Lady. Like Saint Thérèse of Lisieux, she realized that even the smallest personal sacrifices were pleasing gifts for God. Teresita said, "I know that of myself I can do nothing; but thanks to my wonderful confidence that the Blessed Virgin is going to make me holy, I am completely certain that I am going to reach great holiness." Later, as a novice, Teresita asked for a copy of the life of her patroness, Saint Thérèse, "the Little Flower."

She told a friend, "I like the little way of Saint Thérèse very much, but for me that way must always go through Mary."

Teresita was not fond of books, and often said school would be fine if there were no books to study. In study hall, she often spent time sketching on her paper or jotting notes rather than working on one of her assignments. At times she would entreat her sister Carmen, "Come on, Chatina, study the lesson for me." Nevertheless, she got along well with her teachers, and her happy nature made her a favorite with the other students. She was elected "best-dressed" of her class, president of the sodality, and captain of the basketball team which won the school championship in 1947. A good dancer, she enjoyed most things a normal Spanish girl her age enjoyed — including the bull fights, although she clapped for the bull as often as for the matador.

Tennis was Teresita's favorite game, but no matter how hard she  tried she usually came in second. By her senior year, she had improved her game so much that everyone felt certain she would win the championship. After the big game, Teresita returned home with such a happy expression that her mother asked if a new champ had been added to the family. Teresita said, "If you consider one who has won a spiritual victory a champion, then you have your champ, but not a tennis champion."

"I have decided to become a saint."

Teresita then told her mother that before the match one of her friends had jokingly said that she was going to order a larger crown for the champion, as Teresita's head would be swelled by her victory. Although the remark was made only in jest, Teresita began to wonder if her desire for the championship might be only vanity. Before the game, Teresita asked Our Lady for whatever would please Jesus. Then at the match she played her best, but she lost. On the way home, Teresita stopped at the church to tell Our Lady that she understood the decision. An old woman was begging at the church door, and Teresita gave her some money. In turn the beggar handed Teresita a card; she carried this with her to Our Lady's altar without glancing at it. As she knelt, the card fluttered to the floor, and she noticed that it had no picture, only a slogan — "Love makes all things easy."

One of Teresita's friends remembers her party days. "Everyone flocked around Tere at a party, especially the boys, because her conversation was sparkling. Tere loved people, and she loved parties. ... I never knew her to miss one."

Once, Teresita promised to pierce a friend's ears for her. She had barely begun when the girl became queasy and fainted. Instead of panicking, the young surgeon took the opportunity of her friend's unconsciousness to finish her work and insert the new earrings. Her calmness and presence of mind had become a hallmark of her personality.

The young teen, lovely in acts as well as looks

One day in May of 1947, Teresita was praying in the chapel with the other students when, almost without knowing what she was saying, she asked the Virgin, "Mother, give me a religious vocation." Later, she confessed to a friend, "When I came out of chapel, I entered a terrible time of fear. I thought, 'What if she takes me seriously and gives me one!'"

But Jesus, who gives everything we ask through Mary, heard her prayer and answered it, making use of human mediation to work out the call. Teresita did not like to read, and when someone gave her a spiritual book she took it only to be polite. Later, Teresita told the story. "As it was May, I wanted to give a sacrifice to Mary, and so with much good will but little interest I began to read it. The book was about all the different vocations in life. When I reached the chapter that dealt with the religious vocation, I realized that this was the best and that it was definitely what I wanted."

With the consent of her confessor, Teresita petitioned the Mother General to be admitted to the Carmelites of Charity. In the same interview, Teresita asked, "Then may I go to the missions in China?"

Teresita at age seventeen

Laughing, the superior replied that she would have to go to the novitiate first. It seemed that Teresita had always wanted to speed up everything. Several times her father had to restrict her use of the car, for she drove too fast to suit him. And many times she asked her aunt how she could become holy more quickly.

On January 7, 1948, Teresita broke the news to her beloved father. After questioning her and realizing that she had a true vocation, he agreed to tell her mother and her brother and sister. For this deeply devout family, the natural sorrow of parting was tempered by the joy that one of their own had been chosen by God. Teresita entered the novitiate of the Carmelites of Charity on February 23, 1948.

Throughout her postulancy and novitiate, Teresita tried hard to overcome even the slightest fault. She was known for her recollection in prayer and her charity to the other sisters. Even during her school days this recollection had been noticed by one of her teachers, Sister Ramona. Sister Ramona tells us that one day, wishing to see exactly how recollected Teresita was, she knelt beside her for ten minutes while she said the Rosary. Later that afternoon she asked Teresita, "Who was the sister kneeling on the *prie-dieu* with you after lunch today?" Teresita replied, "No one knelt on the *prie-dieu* while I was say-

"Mother, may all who look at me see you."

ing the Rosary, Sister. At least, I don't remember anyone." Teresita, or Sister Maria Teresa, liked nothing better than to keep Mary in all phases of her life.

In May of 1949, Teresita became ill with a bronchial disorder, and her father came to the convent to persuade her superiors to send her home with him for treatment. They decided to wait a few days. Teresita seemed to recover after a dose of streptomycin, so she was allowed to stay to continue her novitiate.

During advent of that year, a group of novices were discussing the coming holy year (1950) and the Pope's intention of proclaiming the dogma of the Assumption. Teresita mentioned that she felt she would be allowed a special favor that year. After much questioning, she admitted that she believed she would be allowed to celebrate the proclamation in heaven.

Some laughed and some protested; none took her very seriously. She replied, "Go on, little sisters, laugh at me. But remember what they always say about the one who laughs last! Every one of you will probably be singing my requiem before the close of 1950. I know I shall be with my Mother on her glorious day. Can you imagine, sisters, what heaven will be like when the dogma of the Assumption is declared?"

"There is very little talk in the schools about the immense benefit that a religious vocation happens to be!"

During the last part of January 1950, Dr. Quevedo was called in to examine Teresita to see what was causing her such severe head and back aches. With a heavy heart, he admitted to the superior that he suspected tubercular meningitis. At the most, she had only a few months to live. Although his natural inclination was to bring his child home, Dr. Quevedo realized that Teresita would be happier to die in God's house. He decided to ask the superior to allow her to stay in the convent. As he was bringing up the subject, Reverend Mother interrupted to ask him if he would please not take Teresita home.

Although she had not completed her novitiate, Teresita was allowed to take her vows to become a fully professed sister. She was also given extreme unction, as her father feared she might lose her mental faculties. Although her mind did wander at periods toward the end, she never totally lost the use of her reason.

Teresita's whole community began to pray for a miraculous recovery. Asked why she was in such a hurry to get to heaven, she replied, "In Heaven, nothing will separate me from Jesus and Mary. Besides, I am of very little use here, but from heaven you will see how busy I shall be."

She told her father, "How would I be afraid to die since I have a Mother in heaven who'll come out to receive me?"

The next three months were filled with pain for Teresita. The only way to relieve the intense agony of the headaches was to draw off some of the spinal fluid by a spinal tap. In all, the doctors punctured her spine a total of sixty-four times. At all times, Teresita attempted to accept the pain without complaint.

Finally, Holy Week of 1950 arrived. On Monday, Teresita was in great pain, and she was in a coma part of Tuesday and Wednesday. She seemed better on Thursday, and asked for a snack in mid-afternoon. A severe spasm of pain hit Thursday evening and left her with a stiff neck

Teresita as a novice

and a headache. She was barely conscious, but fought having another spinal
tap, although it would have provided
some relief, on Holy Saturday, the community began to chant the prayers for
the dying. "Pray for her," the community intoned. "Pray for me," came the
weak response.

Teresita was allowed to take her vows and was dressed, in death, as a fully professed Carmelite of Charity although she had not completed her novitiate

Around eleven in the evening,
Teresita suddenly smiled and looked up.
"How beautiful, O Mary, how beautiful you are." The sisters looked
wonderingly at each other. Did Teresita see the Blessed Mother? Or
was she merely thinking of things soon to be? Teresita gave a final soft
sigh, and then quietly passed away.

Before her death, Dr. Quevedo had asked Teresita to pray for her
mother, as she was taking her daughter's illness very hard. Teresita
promised the first thing she would do when she got to heaven was to
ask God to send complete resignation to her mother. Told of Teresita's
death, Dr. Quevedo was immediately conformed to God's will.

Teresita's cause for canonization is in Rome. She was declared
venerable in 1983. ✝

28

Venerable Zepherin Namuncura
Argentina & Italy, 1886–1905

"Little Chief" of the Araucanos

The Araucano *cacique* (leader) Manuel Namuncura stood in front of Salesian Father Dominic Milanesio. This priest was the Araucanos' friend and the only white man Manuel would trust. Abruptly, he handed the startled priest his two-year-old son. The chief told Father Milanesio to do what was needed to bring the child up in the white man's religion.

The baby was given the baptismal name of Zepherin in honor of a third-century pope-martyr. The name means "wind," and perhaps the priest hoped that this new leader of the Araucano would be a cooling wind to put out the flame of war in his people.

Shortly before Zepherin's birth, the Araucano, under the leadership of Manuel Namuncura, had engaged in a last fierce war against the European colonists. Many atrocities were committed by both sides. At last, the Argentine Minister of War, General Roca, determined to raise a strong army and wipe out the Araucanos. In a swift campaign, the army captured two thousand of the Indians, including Manuel Namuncura's wife and four of his children.

Surrender was the Indians' only alternative to complete destruction. Through the arbitration of the one European the *cacique* would trust, Father Milanesio, a treaty was made, giving the tribe land and making their chief a colonel in the Argentine army. Although the Indians tried to adjust to their new life and the white man's ways, they were decimated by war, disease, and poverty. The treaty was broken in 1894, and the government pushed the Indians further west to worse territory near Alumine, a high valley among the snowy peaks of the Andes Mountains.

Zepherin Namuncura was destined from early childhood to be the *cacique* of his people, the Araucano Indians of the Argentine Pampas.

163

The office was hereditary by family, but did not necessarily fall to the oldest son. Zepherin was the eighth of twelve children of the chief, Manuel Namuncura, and was slated by virtue of his intelligence and ability to be a leader of this fierce, warlike tribe. Instead, however, Zepherin spent his short life training for a different kind of leadership. His burning ambition was to lead his people to the one true God.

In 1897, Manuel Namuncura decided to exercise his rights as a colonel in the army and took the eleven-year-old Zepherin and demanded his enrollment at the army academy, El Tigre. It was the chief's wish that there the boy could learn the white man's military tactics. Unfortunately, as Zepherin was the only Indian child at the school, the other students were cruel in their treatment of him. He was so unhappy there that he began to lose weight and actually became ill. At the suggestion of Father Dominic, he was moved to the Salesian mission school in Buenos Aires.

At the mission school, Zepherin studied hard, and his grades remained in the top half of the class. Though not particularly bright when it came to books, he was, in the words of his teacher, a "plugger."

The young Zepherin

Although the schedules and the discipline were hard on a boy used to the freedom of the Indian tribal existence, he felt at home among the students. Asked what he liked best about the school, he replied, "The Church and the food," although he complained that he wasn't allowed to eat the "bread" at the altar. In September of 1898, however, the "Little Chief" was finally allowed to partake of this Food, when he made his First Communion at the age of twelve. Zepherin considered this event to be entering into a lifelong treaty. Having agreed to meet Our Lord, he bound himself to live as a son of God.

One day during class, his teacher noticed that Zepherin often appeared to be daydreaming and staring out into the corridor. But despite the fact that the teacher called on him suddenly several times, he could not catch the boy without a ready reply. For Zepherin, time in the classroom was restrictive, like a prison. Later, the teacher moved Zepherin to a new seat where he could not stare off into the corridor. After class, Zepherin asked to be returned to his former place. When asked why, he replied, "From the old place, I could see through the window the sanctuary lamp in the chapel. When I could no longer stay still and the hours seemed to drag on endlessly, I looked up there and asked Our Lord for the strength to carry on. From the new place I can't see the lamp anymore. Now it will be tougher for me."

A child of the outdoors, Zepherin loved sports. He was a good horseman and an expert archer. His clever hands were often occupied in making bows and arrows for himself and his classmates, and sometimes the boys would have archery competitions with "Zeph" as the judge. When they tired of playing, Zepherin would lead them into the chapel for prayer.

One time, when Zepherin's father came for a visit to his son, he was treated as an honored guest, and the two spent several happy days together. When Manuel left, he gave Zepherin the sum of ten pesos with instructions to use it for a special treat for himself.

Like most of the boys at the mission school, Zepherin was poor. His clothes were usually hand-me-downs, and ten pesos would buy something quite nice. The priest was surprised when, as soon as his father had left, Zepherin brought him the money, telling him to use it to decorate Our Lady's altar. The priest protested that the money was intended for Zepherin. In turn, Zepherin replied that, used for Our Lady, it would indeed be a treat for him. He often stated that he wanted Our Lady to become the queen of his people.

Although his outgoing personality and basic honesty made him a favorite at the school, sometimes the boys would unintentionally say things that would hurt Zepherin's feelings. Once, when a fellow student in a discussion about the Indians asked Zeph what human flesh tasted like, the boy bowed his head and a large tear slipped down his high cheeks. He did not remonstrate with the thoughtless student, however, but simply continued the conversation and ignored the question.

As the time for Zepherin to leave the mission school grew closer, he was asked what he wanted to do. He said that he wanted to become a priest in order to take the true religion to his people, and to open a school for the children of the Araucano. Bishop Cagliero, the Salesian superior, liked this sturdy seventeen-year-old, and after warning him that studies for the priesthood would not be easy, arranged for his entrance into the minor seminary at Viedma.

At the seminary, too, Zepherin was well-liked. He engaged in sports and small hunting expeditions for recreation, as well as studying hard enough to become second in his class. He also enjoyed doing card tricks for his classmates. Zepherin remembered the words of the priest who had come to convert his people: "Serve God with joy."

In addition to the fun and the studying, Zepherin was growing in virtue. He could often be found in front of the Blessed Sacrament, praying for his people. The "Little Chief" did not forget his Indian origins; he wanted to remain an Indian. A favorite devotion was the Rosary — also prayed for the benefit of his people. One of his classmates later said, "During the six months I lived with Namuncura, I saw him relive all the virtues I had read about in the life of Dominic Savio."

On September 24, 1903, with the permission of his superiors,

Venerable Zepherin Namuncura,
true son of Argentina

Zepherin organized a procession in honor of Our Lady of Mercy. That night he fell into bed tired from his day's labor. He awoke coughing and spitting up blood. The disease that was slowly wiping out his entire tribe had caught up with him; Zepherin had tuberculosis.

On being informed of Namuncura's condition, the bishop immediately had him sent to the hospital at Viedma. Of his time there, the hospital chaplain said, "'Little Chief' rarely talked. We often thought he lived in continual prayer. He never gave signs of impatience or disgust. Grateful for any service, he smiled his thanks to all and obeyed every order given him."

In April of 1904, Pope Pius X appointed Bishop Cagliero archbishop, and summoned him to Rome. The bishop asked Zepherin if he would like to accompany him to Rome and remain there to continue his studies for the priesthood. Perhaps the warm dry air of the region would be better for his health.

After a month at sea, the bishop and the young seminarian set foot on European soil. Zepherin was impressed with the strangeness of everything, but the biggest attraction was the large picture of Mary Help of Christians in the basilica at Turin. The picture seemed like a magnet, drawing the young Indian to pray before it for help for his people.

The priest who took care of Zepherin while he was in Turin said, "Every time I looked for him, I found him praying before the picture of Mary Help of Christians." Asked what he was praying for, his constant reply was, "For my people."

At Turin, and later in Rome, Zepherin was privileged to have several exceptional experiences. He was present for the translation of the remains of Saint John Bosco, and in company with Archbishop Cagliero, had a private audience with Pope Pius X. During a large mission exhibit in Turin, a well-dressed lady stopped by Zepherin's booth. He had dressed in his native costume for the exhibit, and his manners and refinement were impressive to all. The lady asked that he guide her through the rest of the exhibit, which he willingly did. What a surprise when he later discovered that the lady was the Queen of Italy!

At first, Zepherin attended a seminary in Turin. The director said of him, "He has a heart warm with God's love. It's a heart of gold, and sees no evil in anyone. It's a treat to hear him talk about God and Our Lady. He loves God like we love our mothers ... warmly, intensely, as though he were always in God's presence." Unfortunately, the Turin climate was not beneficial to his health, so he transferred to the Salesian boarding school of Villa Sora near Rome on the Alban hills. His fellow students had a deep respect for this quiet and somewhat withdrawn young man. "I never saw him smile; he was always serious, almost sad. Yet his eyes were always serene and smiling," remembered one of the students. Another recalled, "In the chapel where he often went to pray, he was recollected like an angel."

In the spring of 1905, Zepherin's health took a sudden turn for the worse. He was racked with cough and fever, and seemed to be often in pain. Nevertheless, the smile in his eyes never left. His director wrote, "He got worse day by day, yet he was never impatient. He suffered, held onto his cross generously."

In Rome, circa 1904

Zepherin wrote to his father, "Don't worry about me. I always have a doctor beside me to look after my health and I'm always with my friend, Msgr. Cagliero." He asked his friends, "Pray that I may get better and, if it is the Lord's will, become a priest."

Zepherin was transferred to the hospital run by the Brothers of God in Rome. Here he bore his cross of suffering patiently, constantly praying the Rosary for his people. He died on the morning of May 11, surrounded by several of the brothers who were praying for him. He was buried in Rome. In 1924, his remains were taken back to his beloved Argentina, and reinterred at the Salesian school of Fortin Mercedes. Pope Paul VI declared Zepherin venerable in 1972. ✝

29

Young Martyrs of China

Saints Andrew Wang Tianqing*, Anna Wang, Chi Zhuze*, Fan Kun, Ji Yu*, John Baptist Wu Mantang, John Zhu Wurui, Magdalen Du Fengju, Mary Zhao, Paolo Lang Fu, Paul Wu Wanshu, Peter Zhu Rixin*, Simon Qin-Qunfu*, Wang Cheng, Zheng Xu

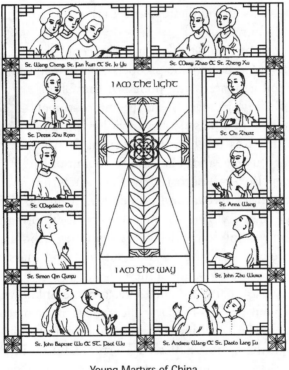

Young Martyrs of China
DRAWING BY THERESA ZHENG

The 120 Blessed Martyrs of China were canonized October 1, 2000, by Pope John Paul II. The martyrs include eighty-seven Chinese nationals, who are the first canonized Chinese saints, and thirty-three foreign missionaries. Fifteen of the martyrs were youth under the age of twenty, with the youngest being only seven years old.

There was also a ten-month-old baby killed in his mother's arms who is not listed as a saint.

Members of the group were beatified in several separate groups. They were executed in China between 1747 and 1947, with most of them being killed during the Boxer Rebellion of 1900.

Religious persecution has occurred at various periods in the history of China. The first recorded persecution was during the early Yuan dynasty (1281-1367). Another series of persecutions happened again at the end of the Ming dynasty (1606-1637). Some missionaries were expelled while others were arrested and executed. During the Ching dynasty (1648-1907), persecutions began again with the local Churches in the south and afterwards in the southwest parts of China.

The 120 martyrs of China

At the turn of the 20th Century, the center of Catholic life in China was the prosperous province of Hebei. Unfortunately, the policy of the Ching dynasty in Beijing, in reaction to the international exploitation of China, was a policy of violent protest against all that was foreign. The uprising by the "Society for Justice and Harmony" (commonly known as the "Boxers") occurred in 1900, when the Boxers, with both approval and cooperation from the Ching dynasty, turned their fanatic violence primarily against all foreign missionaries and their faithful. They destroyed churches, schools, and everything that represented the foreign religion, and massacred nearly 30,000 Christians, almost all Chinese.

The names of many of China's martyrs are unknown. Rev. Fang Ho worked from 1937 to 1945 to collect relics of the martyrs and take them to Taipei, Taiwan. Since that time, they have been displayed for veneration in the Chinese Blessed Martyrs Church in Peng Chiao. The long-awaited canonization of these Chinese martyrs was a great event in the history of the Chinese Church. The martyrs will undoubtedly be an encouragement to those in China who are still suffering persecution.

Saint John Baptist Wu Mantang
1883–1900

Saint Paul Wu Wanshu,
1884–1900

Wu Mantang and Wu Wanshu, along with seven members of their family, were led by their grandfather to Xiaoluyi Village in June, 1900, in an attempt to escape the persecution and find refuge from the Boxers. When a band of Boxers approached the village, they were discovered in their hiding place in some bushes. They were questioned and told that if they admitted to being Christians they would be killed. They responded, "You may kill us, but we will remain Catholic Christians forever." John Wu was tortured, but he continued to pray: "As long as my lips can move, they will pray and lift up praises to the Lord." They were killed on the spot.

Saint Simon Qin-Qunfu*
1886–1900

Simon was from the village of Nanpeiluo in Hebei Province. He was martyred along with his widowed mother, Elizabeth, and three of his five brothers and sisters: Matthew Qin Guozhen, Paul Qin Baolu, Anna, Mary and Francisca. Matthew and Francisca escaped.

In June of 1900, the family fled to Liucun. Here, a rich man wanted Simon to marry his daughter, promising them protection from the Boxers. But Simon said: "Mother, do not deem my bodily life worth more than my soul. I have decided not to leave you. If we die,

| Saint John Baptist Wu Mantang, age seventeen | Saint Paul Wu Wanshu, age sixteen | Saint Simon Qin-Qunfu, age fourteen |

we die together!" With that, the rich man informed the Boxers where the family was. When the Boxers caught up to them on July 17, Simon asked them to let the others go. He knelt down and prayed. Without hesitation, the pursuers killed him and wounded his brother, Paul. After Simon's death, people from Liucun came to bury him and carried Paul to his own home in Peiluo. However, in Peiluo, Paul had to hide in the cemetery for a day and a half in smoldering ashes. The Boxers later found Paul and nailed him to a tree.

On July 19, the women were caught, taken back to the village and asked to deny God and get married. Bravely, the women answered "We are God's daughters and keep our virginity for life. We believe in Him and there is no way to change our minds. Whether you kill us or not is your own business, but it is impossible for us to deny our faith." They were taken to a field outside the village where a crowd of women stood. Saint Elizabeth said to them, "Please go home; what will happen to us will frighten you. As for us, God will reward us with eternal life, so we are not afraid of death because to die is to return home." Mary began to cry out, so Elizabeth held her hand, telling her not to be afraid. They were shot while standing in a pear garden. Francisca was whisked out of the crowd by a relative and saved from death.

Saint Anna Wang
1886–1900

Saint Andrew Wang Tianqing*
1891–1900

On July 21, 1900, several Catholics from Wei County, Hebei Province, were arrested by Boxer bandits at the gate of the village. Joseph, the fervent leader of the Catholics in that village, was the first to be killed. The other three were locked up in a room where they spent the night in prayer. They were called the next day to either give up their faith or die. These four martyrs, including Saint Andrew Wang Tianqing and Saint Anna Wang, were killed after refusing to renounce their faith. The brave girl responded, "I believe in God. I am a Christian. I do not renounce God. Jesus save me!"

Anna Wang, fourteen, is perhaps the most famous and beloved of all the Chinese martyrs. She was born to Christian parents in 1886 in southern Hebei Province. Her mother died when she was only five and her father later remarried. When she was eleven, she was promised in marriage, but she vigorously opposed the proposal.

After her refusal to apostatize, Anna's martyrdom became even more difficult because her father and stepmother, although baptized Catholics, were willing to apostatize to avoid death and kept begging Anna to do the same. In front of guards, Anna pleaded with her step-

Saint Anna
Wang,
age fourteen

mother not to abandon the faith. After the last of such scenes, her stepmother walked away, leaving Anna in grief but even more determined to remain faithful until the end.

During the last day and night, the beautiful child was a model of inspiration to all the prisoners. In the center of the floor she remained kneeling with dignity, calm and confident, strengthening the others. Even the guards and Boxers admired her composure. They tried in every way to make her recant, including promising her everything good, including a fine marriage.

After taking the martyrs to the place of execution, as the soldiers walked forward for the execution, one of them gave her a last chance to recant. At first, she was silent, but when he became insistent, she said, "Do not touch me. I am a Christian. I prefer to die rather than to give up my faith."

Saint Andrew
Wang Tianqing,
age nine

The soldier cut off her right arm and asked again, "Do you deny your religion?" Anna was silent, and when the soldier struck her again she said, "The door of heaven is open." She whispered the name of Jesus three times and lowered her head. She was finally beheaded, but witnesses said that even after her head had fallen, Anna remained kneeling in prayer until the guards pushed her body to the floor.

After Anna's heroic death, her stepmother repented of her own faithlessness and returned to a fervent practice of the faith.

Saint Andrew Wang Tianqing was executed at the same time as Anna Wang. Some non-Christians at the scene wanted to save the little boy, but his mother cried out "I am a Christian, my son is a Christian. You will have to kill us both." Little Andrew knelt down and smiled at his mother while the executioner cut off his head with an ax. That same day, five women were killed with their children, including a ten-month-old baby.

Saint Peter Zhu Rixin*
1881–1900

One of the most tragic incidents was the massacre of the entire Christian population at Zhujiahe of Qin County, in the province of Hebei. Originally a Catholic center with 300 believers, it was also a walled town that could be defended against the persecutors. Many faithful had fled from their homes to find refuge there. By May 1900, around 3,000 Christians were gathered at this village. Rev. Leon Ignace Mangin, Rev. Tang Ailing (Paul Denn, S.J.), and Rev. Stephen Ren worked hard to bolster the town defenses. More importantly, however, they prepared the people for martyrdom, and they were kept busy by hearing the confessions of the people. On July 15, 1900, the Boxers, reinforced by 10,000 imperial soldiers, attacked the village, which was fortified by only 1,000 Christians. Despite the overwhelming odds, the town resisted the attack for three days, leaving many dead or wounded. Many escaped, but most were still present when the Boxers and imperial army marched into town and began killing men, women, and children alike.

Saint Peter Zhu Rixin, age nineteen

The town's cathedral was filled, but the Boxers opened fire on the people, then set the building ablaze, killing the priests and the devoted Christians who were trapped inside. Those who escaped by jumping out of the windows were stabbed to death outside. Fifty one Christians were caught and set for execution the following day.

General Chen, the leader of the Boxers, tried to persuade them to apostatize, but all except two of them remained steady in the Faith. Among the faithful was Saint Peter Zhu Rixin. Zhu Rixin had been born in the predominantly Catholic village of East Zhujiahe, in Qin County, Hebei Province, and baptized with the name Peter. He studied at a school near Lou Village and was considered a promising student.

The general did his best to persuade the handsome and promising Peter Zhu. Finally, to silence the judge once and for all, he asked him firmly, "Would you deny your mother and father? If you would not do that, much less will I deny my Father, my God." Angered at the sturdy faith of the young Catholic, the general gave the final order to behead him.

Saint John Zhu Wurui
1883–1900

Saint John Zhu Wurui, age seventeen

John Zhu Wurui was born and baptized in the Green Grass River Village, Qin County, Hebei Province. On August 18, 1900, his village was besieged by the Boxers, and John slipped away to warn other Catholic villages. He was caught on the way and arrested by the County Prefect. He was interrogated but stood firm in his faith and was handed over to the Boxers to be executed. They beheaded him and hung his head on a tree as a warning to other Catholics.

Saint Magdalen Du Fengju
1881–1900

Saint Magdalen Du Fengju, age nineteen

On June 29th, during a raid, Magdalen, along with her mother, two brothers, and a sister, was discovered hiding in a pit covered with reeds near the village. Magdalen and her sister ran to a friend's house, but Magdalen arrived too late and found that the door was shut when she arrived. She sat there and awaited her fate. When the Boxers saw her, they shot and wounded her. Her mother and brothers had refused to apostatize, so they were killed.

While the villagers were digging a ditch to bury her mother and brothers, an old friend of the family found Magdalen Du still alive. He quietly asked her to apostatize to save her life, but she retorted: "Impossible! I want to go to heaven and be happy with my mother and brothers!" The Boxers threw them all into the ditch. Magdalen peacefully took her place among them, pushing the bodies of her mother and brothers to one side. She covered her face with her sleeves and was buried alive at the age of nineteen.

Saint Paolo Lang Fu
1893–1900

When the Boxers invaded the Lu Village, Qinghe County, Hebei Province, on July 16, 1900, they caught Mrs. Mary Lang-Yang, tied her to a tree, and began to question her about her faith. Returning from playing outdoors, Lang Fu saw his mother tied up and began to cry. She simply said, "Don't cry son, come here." The Boxers then set fire to their house, pierced her body with a lance, and cut off the boy's arm. Both were thrown into the fire.

Saint Paolo Lang Fu, age seven

Saint Chi Zhuze*
1882–1900

In 1882, Chi Zhuze was born to a simple and honest peasant family in the village of Dezhaoin, Shen County, Hebei Province. Moved by the good example of the Catholics in his village, he learned about the Catholic faith and decided to enter the Church at the age of seventeen.

Although he was illiterate, Chi Zhuze made great efforts to learn Catholic doctrine and attended Mass every Sunday with the other students. By the fall of 1899, when the Boxer Rebellion reached its height, his parents objected and said, "If you want to remain a member of this family, stop going to church and wait until the rebellion has ended." However, Chi Zhuze remained firm in his faith in spite of his family's opposition. On New Year's Eve, he refused to worship the family idols and was banished from the family, enduring all hardships cheerfully in the name of God.

Saint Chi Zhuze, age eighteen

In June of 1900, the Boxers became more aggressive against the Catholics, who began to dig trenches and arm themselves for self-defense. Strangers were admitted into their village only after careful screening. Since Zhuze was not yet baptized, he was not known in Catholic circles and was turned away when he sought shelter there.

Finally, he found one Catholic who knew him, took him in and gave him a job as a servant in his house.

A short time later, his parents discovered his refuge and ordered him to return home. With filial piety, Zhuze went home. On the way he met some Boxers who ordered him to worship idols in a nearby temple. He refused to do so and courageously told them he was a Catholic. Then they began to torture him by cutting off his arm. He told them, "Do with me what you wish. Courage, go on. Cut me in as many pieces as you wish and you will see that every piece is a Catholic." He remained firm and the mutilation continued. Some of the villagers went to notify his parents but they didn't try to save him. After his death, the first fruit of his martyrdom was that his family became Catholic.

Saint Wang Cheng
1882–1900

Saint Fan Kun
1884–1900

Saint Ji Yu (Chi Yu)*
1885–1900

Saint Zheng Xu
1889–1900

Wang Cheng, baptized with the name Lucy, was born in Laochuntan Village, Nengxin County. Fan Kun and Ji Ui were both baptized with the name Mary, and both were from Daji Village in Wuqiao County. Zheng Xu was born in Kou Village, Dongguang County, and was also baptized with the name Mary. All of these places were located in Hebei Province. The four girls grew up in the orphanage in Wangla Village, which was founded by the parish priest there.

On June 24, 1900, the Boxers invaded that village, burnt down the church, and killed all the Catholics. They saved the four orphan girls with something else in mind for them. They first took them to Yingjia, then to Mazetang. Their leader, Ying Zheng, made a proposal of marriage to Wang Cheng, but after four days of persuasion, she rejected it, considering a marriage to a leader of the Boxers as a betrayal of her faith and of God. At the same time, the Boxers were trying to force

Saint Wang
Cheng,
age eighteen

Saint Fan Kun,
age sixteen

Saint Ji Yu,
age fifteen

Saint Zheng Xu,
age eleven

Kan Fun to marry another Boxer, but this incident brought a rebuke from the whole group. Their mission was to arrest Catholics and kill those who refused to apostatize, not to marry them. Intimidated, they took the four girls back to Mala village. The three younger ones began to cry during this trip, but Wang Cheng spoke up to encourage them saying, "Don't cry, we are going to heaven soon. God has given us life, and He will take it back. We should not be reluctant givers, but offer ourselves cheerfully." To the torturers, she said, "God will punish you for this some day."

For the rest of the trip back to Mala, the Boxers abused them with words of contempt for the Church and for God. However, the courage shown by Wang Cheng strengthened the faith of the three younger ones. When they arrived at Wangla Village, they were ordered to get out of the cart and to reconsider their attitude, but all four unanimously refused to apostatize, saying, "No! We are daughters of God. We will not betray Him." At that, the four girls were murdered.

Saint Mary Zhao
1883–1900

Saint Mary
Zhao,
age seventeen

Mary, her mother, and her sister Rosa, a catechist, were from Zhaojiacun, Wuchiao County, Hebei Province.

On July 28, 1900, all three women tried to hide from a pursuing band of Boxers by jumping into a well. The Boxers dragged them from the well and attempted to force them to deny their faith. Rosa answered them with a clear resolution: "We have already made up our minds that we would rather die then deny our faith." Then she turned to her mother and sister, telling them to pray to Jesus, asking for help and strength to give up their lives for the faith. At that moment, a man named Zhao Wuhai implored the Boxers to spare their lives. But Rosa told him, "Uncle, don't waste your time trying to save us. Since we want to keep our faith, we are happy to die for it." Then she told the Boxers: "This is not a proper place for execution. If you want to kill us, take us to the cemetery where our ancestors are buried and kill us there."

The Boxers took them to the Zhao family cemetery, where they not only decapitated them, but also burned their bodies to ashes.

*Several transliterations of the names of the martyrs may lead to some confusion in their names. For example: Saint Simon Qin-Qunfu is listed in some other sources as Qin-Cunfu; Saint Ji Yu is also listed as Chi Yu; Saint Peter Zhu Rixin is sometimes called Peter Tchou; Saint Chi Zhuze is also known as Si; Tianqing is also spelled Tianquing. ✣

30

Young Martyrs of Korea

Saints Agatha Yi, Barbara Yi*, Joseph Cho Yun-ho,
Peter Yu Tae-ch'ol

On May 6, 1984, in Seoul, Korea, in the first canonization to take place outside of Rome since the thirteenth century, Pope John Paul II named 103 new saints on what he called the "happiest day, the greatest feast, in the whole history of the Church in Korea." These 103 martyrs are representative of the approximately 10,000 Christians martyred in Korea over a period lasting almost 130 years. Youth are not lacking in this list; four of the martyrs were younger than twenty years of age.

That same year, the Catholic Church in Korea celebrated its bicentennial. Two hundred years earlier, in 1784, a young Korean scholar, Lee Sung-hoon, had traveled to Peking and been baptized into the Catholic Church. He then returned to his homeland with a number of religious books and articles, as well as a spark of faith which was to ignite the fires of Christianity in the land of Korea.

Korea is the only country in the history of the Church which initiated its own evangelization. It began with the efforts of a group of Korean scholars who studied the Christian Faith from the books that Lee Sung-hoon had brought back from China. These lay Koreans became convinced that they needed a priest. They sent an envoy to Peking requesting one, and in 1795 Father Chu Mun-mo, a priest of the Peking diocese, became the first missionary priest to Korea. Father Chu Mun-mo was martyred, after six years of labor, in the persecution of 1801–1802, which also cost the lives of over 300 of the converts.

Repeated appeals for another priest were made to Peking and to Rome, and at last, in 1831, a deeply impressed Vatican responded by committing priests of the Paris Foreign Mission Society to work in the Church in Korea. Father Pierre Philibert Maubant made the long and difficult journey across China to Korea and arrived in Seoul in 1836. Once there, he began ministering to the Christians in hiding.

Bishop Lanrent Joseph Marie Imbert was appointed vicar apostolic, and arrived in Korea in 1837. Then a third missionary arrived.

In 1839, a new persecution arose. Bishop Imbert and his two colleagues surrendered themselves to the authorities, hoping that this might avert some of the official wrath from the faithful. The three were tortured and executed, along with numbers of Korean Christians, both men and women. Others were imprisoned or exiled.

Saint Barbara Yi*
Circa 1824–1839

Yi Barbara was born in the Ch'ong-p'a district of Seoul. She was orphaned at an early age and brought up by her aunts Barbara and Magdalene, who later also became martyrs for the Faith. Testimony as to her character records that she seemed like one of those souls who is given to the world to love God and win heaven in the shortest possible time. She was only fifteen when she was arrested.

At first she was taken to police headquarters where she was tortured innumerable times. Then, she was transferred to the criminal court, where she resisted the judge who tried by threats and cajoling to get her to give up her faith. He was unable to obtain a single word or the slightest sign of weakness from her. Touched with pity, the judge sent her back to the petty offenders court as too young to come before the criminal court.

Saint Barbara Yi

Barbara was thrown into a prison cell with three young boys about her age. They spent their time encouraging one another. Barbara contracted typhoid fever from the unhealthy and filthy conditions in the jail; after a week of intense pain, she died on May 27, 1839.

Saint Peter Yu Tae-ch'ol
Circa 1826-1839

Yu Tae-ch'ol Peter was the son of the martyr Yu Chin-gil Augustine and a pagan mother. His mother tried very hard to hinder her son in the practice of his faith and make him offer sacrifices to the ancestors. When his mother and sister asked him why he wouldn't obey his mother, Peter gently replied that he couldn't disobey the Heavenly King, Father of all creatures. In all other matters except faith, Peter obeyed his mother faithfully and tried not to offend his family.

When the persecutions broke out, Peter was filled with an ardent desire to be a martyr. He was deeply moved by the heroic example of his imprisoned father and the other martyrs, and at last he couldn't control his love for God. In July, 1839, he gave himself up to the government authorities and was put in prison. When taken before the court, Peter was persuaded, threatened, and tortured but would not deny God.

One day a prison guard hit Peter hard on his leg with a long tobacco pipe, and a piece of flesh was torn off. The guard asked him if he still believed in God. Peter answered, "Yes, I certainly do. I am not afraid of being hit." The guard then threatened to put a burning charcoal into Peter's mouth, so Peter opened his mouth wide and said that he was ready. Because the young boy of thirteen was so brave, the guard couldn't bring himself to put the charcoal in his mouth. Another day, Peter was beaten so severely that he fainted. When his fellow prisoners helped him recover consciousness, he told them, "Don't worry. I will not die because of this pain."

Saint Peter Yu Tae-ch'ol with his father, Augustine, also a martyr

Peter was interrogated fourteen times and tortured on that many occasions. He was whipped with 600 lashes of the rod and beaten with a "robber's plank," a cudgel,

Saint Peter Yu
Tae-ch'ol

forty-five strokes. His whole body was covered with wounds, his bones were broken, and flesh was torn off. In spite of this, witnesses testify that he always had a happy, smiling face. Peter's love of God seemed to change his face and ridicule the torturing adults. No one could believe that such a young boy had been so severely tortured, but there were ten witnesses who gave sworn testimony to these facts and to Peter's courage.

The government officials had felt that Peter would die from his beatings but he didn't. Therefore, they strangled him to death on October 31, 1839. He is the youngest of the 103 Korean martyr saints.

Saint Agatha Yi
Circa 1823–1840

Yi Agatha was put in prison along with her father, Yi Augustine, and her mother, Kwon Barbara, on April 8, 1839. The police chief tried to persuade her to renounce her faith, and she was repeatedly interrogated and tortured. Since this was not successful, he used violent means to force her to surrender. He was surprised that even violence was not effective. The young girl endured the tortures and threats so courageously that the people around her could hardly believe the strength of divine grace working in this seventeen-year-old girl.

Saint Agatha Yi
(facing right with her hand up)

The guards lied to her and told her that her parents had given up their faith and had been released from prison. Agatha answered for herself and for her younger brother Damian, saying, "Whether or not my parents denied their religion is their affair. As for us, we cannot betray the Lord of heaven, whom we have always served."

It was a miracle that Agatha was able to preserve her virginity, living among the prison guards who were like beasts. She was whipped 300 lashes with the rod, and beaten ninety strokes with a club. All these sufferings, along with thirst, hunger, and sickness did not discourage her. Constantly Agatha thought of her father, beheaded on May 24, and her mother, martyred on September 3. She was determined to imitate their example of Christian fidelity.

After nine months of imprisonment, Agatha was sentenced to death by strangulation. The executioners came on January 9, 1840, and seized her in her cell. They took her to a special room, put the cord around her neck and tugged at it for a long time, finally tying the ends of the cord to upright stakes.

In 1845 Bishop Jean Joseph Ferreol, after several attempts to enter the country, was at last successful. In the meantime, contact had been established between the Christians and the outer world by a young Korean student for the priesthood, Andrew Kim, who went back and forth between the Christian groups and his ecclesiastical superiors. Father Kim was ordained in 1845, and shortly thereafter became a victim of the anti-Christian policy of his government; he was beheaded in 1846.

Immediately prior to his martyrdom, Father Kim wrote a letter to the faithful, urging them to accept persecution as an act of God's providence. He told his flock that the Church in Korea could be no exception in a Church founded on the sufferings of our Lord and spread by the sufferings of the Apostles.

The decade following Bishop Ferreol's arrival in 1845 marked a period of rapid growth for the Church in Korea. Korea now had 12 priests and 23,000 believers. In 1866, a final violent persecution broke out. Two Bishops and seven other missionaries were executed. Three missionaries escaped by fleeing the country. By September of 1868, 2,000 of the Christians had perished. From among these come the additional martyrs adding up to 103.

Saint Joseph Cho Yun-ho
1848–1866

Cho Yun-ho Joseph was born in 1848 in Ch'ung-ch'ong Province. In 1864, he came to Chon-ju and got married. The young couple lived with his parents, and the family did their best to follow Christian teaching. Joseph's faith was very deep and he observed all the church regulations faithfully.

Cho Yun-ho Joseph was just coming home when his father was arrested. Peter asked his son to run away, but Joseph gave himself up. Both father and son encouraged each other not to abandon the faith.

Joseph told his interrogators that his grandfather had taught him the Catholic Faith. He also told them that he didn't have any Catholic books. They tortured him severely to make him deny his faith but he didn't succumb. He was sent to the Chon-ju prison with his father.

Saint Joseph Cho Yun-ho (second from right)

There was a Korean national law forbidding the simultaneous execution of father and son, so his father was executed first. As they parted, Joseph told his father, "You are going to the place of eternal bliss. Don't forget me when you are there." His father replied, "Of course, I am going to die. Still you should not be weak; don't fail to follow me."

When exhorted to apostatize, Joseph calmly replied, "Whether I live or die is not a matter under your authority, so don't say anything more about it." This, of course, brought more torture, even on his way to the execution ground. The executioner ran fast, pulling the wooden board around Joseph's neck, to make him tired.

Joseph ate his last meal at the execution site, making the sign of the cross very devoutly before eating. At the last exhortation just before his execution, he persevered in his faith answering, "Suppose one's parents commit a crime and in lieu of them one is arrested. On this occasion, do you think a judge can possibly tell one to renounce and disavow one's parents? I have come to know the good teaching of the Heavenly God and have followed it. Then how can I say that it is false and discard it? I can never do that, so put me to death right away."

On December 18, 1866, under the bridge in the market place outside the West Gate in Chon-ju, Joseph was beaten to death with sixteen blows of the cudgel. He was only nineteen years old. Joseph's mother and a large crown of onlookers were at the site of his martyrdom and after his death his body was interred in the same place as his father's. Thus, three generations of this family — Joseph, his father, and his grandfather — had the honor of being martyrs.

Despite the fact that 10,000 Korean Christians had been martyred, the Foreign Mission Society of Paris would not be discouraged. Again and again, attempts were made to place missionaries in the hostile country. In 1876, two French priests were led into the country by Korean guides, and in 1877, a new bishop entered the country. He was Felix Clair Ridel, one of the priests who had escaped the persecution of 1866. Bishop Ridel was arrested, but French pressure on China and Japan obtained his release.

The Korean martyrs

A new anti-Christian law was issued in 1881, but it was not strictly enforced, and the persecutions were formally ended in 1882 by a treaty with the United States. In 1886, a treaty with France gave protection, and even a somewhat favored status, to both missionaries and their converts. Thus, the persecutions of the Christian missionaries became a thing of the past. At that time there were five priests and 12,500 Catholics in Korea.

After nearly a hundred years, marked by some 10 periods of persecution of varying degrees of severity, the "seed of Christians," the blood of countless known and unknown Christian Korean martyrs, finally began to yield its harvest. Today the church is alive and thriving in South Korea.

*Several transliterations of the names of the Korean martyrs may lead to some confusion in their names. For example: one source says Yi Barbara, while another has Barbara Lee. ✛

31

Young Martyrs of Mexico

José Sánchez del Río and Saint David Roldán Lara

The Catholic Church has flourished in Mexico since it was introduced there in the 1500s. Despite this, it has also faced periods of brutal persecution. Between 1915 and 1937, severe restrictions were placed on the Church, including bans on Church ownership of property, expulsion of the papal legate and other priests and nuns, and executions of Catholics.

———

José Sánchez del Río
1913–1928

Bravery when facing death is not a trait reserved for adults. From the time of the earliest Christians, the Church has numbered youthful martyrs among the ranks of the saints. Close to our own time, José Sánchez del Río, the "Boy Soldier," fought and died bravely in his battle for Christ the King.

José was born March 28, 1913, in Villa de Sahuayo, Michoacan, Mexico, the son of Don Macario Sánchez and Doña Maria del Río. He was baptized when he was only a week old in the parish church. He began school in his hometown of Sahuayo, and later attended school in Guadalajara.

In 1926, President Calles was making every effort to stamp out the Catholic Church in Mexico. He passed a number of laws which took freedom of religion away from the Mexican people. At first, the Catholics tried peaceful means to change the laws, but their efforts were ignored. At last, they could stand no more and they took up arms in what is known as the "*Cristero* Rebellion." José's older brothers, Miguel and Macario, were inflamed with the Christian ideals of Anacleto González Flores, the chief of the A.C.J.M. (Association of Young Mexican Catholics) in Guadalajara. In August, they joined the forces of General Cristerio Sánchez Ramirez.

José, who was only thirteen years old and an aspirant (junior associate) of the A.C.J.M., wanted to follow in the footsteps of his brothers. Because of his young age, the General would not allow him to join the fight. José begged to be allowed to be a young soldier for Christ the King. His mother, of course, objected, saying that he might be killed. "Mama, do not let me lose the opportunity to gain heaven so easily and so soon," he replied.

He wrote to General Mendoza several times, pleading, "If I am not able to handle a gun, I may be helpful in other ways, such as taking care of the horses or carrying water and ammunition." And in ingenuously simple language he added, "And besides, I know how to fry *alubias* [beans]."

At last Ruben Guizar Morfin, who commanded the forces near Cotija, accepted him in his ranks. Immediately, the little rookie demonstrated his valor in this new crusade. Because of his religious fervor, and his ardent desire to defend the faith, he was named the flag bearer of the troops. He became a favorite of the troops, who called him with affection "Tarcisio," after Saint Tarsicius, the young "Martyr of the Eucharist."

What was the secret of José's courage and strong wish to defend the faith? Daily Communion, just like the martyrs of the early Christian centuries. In addition, he had often gone to the tomb of the first martyr of the A.C.J.M., Joachim Silva, begging for the courage to be a good soldier for Christ.

In a fierce battle on February 5, 1928, the General's horse was shot. On seeing this, like a true veteran, José leapt off his own horse and offered it to the General, saying, "My General, take my horse and save yourself. If they kill me, I won't be missed, but you would!" Then the young soldier crawled to a strategic position and began shooting until he used his last cartridge. Then, taking his empty gun to use as a weapon, he raced toward the enemy like a little demon. He was captured and taken before the commander of the government forces. Calmly he said, "Here I am because I am out of bullets, but I don't surrender to you."

The soldiers formed around him with their rifles raised, ready to shoot him, but the commander would not allow the execution because he saw how young the valiant little soldier of Christ the King was. Instead, he determined to incorporate the boy into the troops of the government. On hearing this, José exclaimed, "I'd rather die. I hate the persecuting government. It is my enemy. Shoot me!"

From Cotija, where he was taken prisoner, José was taken to

José Sánchez del Río

his home town of Sahuayo, and put in the sacristy of the church as his jail. The General hoped that either by coaxing or threatening he might get some information from José. Here the *federales* had stabled their horses and the deputy had made a pen for his fighting cocks. José prayed all night. In the morning, he realized that the chickens had been put in the church. Angered that the *federales* had desecrated the church, he wrung the necks of the chickens. When the deputy found what he had done, he asked the boy why he had killed the fighting cocks. Indignantly, José responded, "The church is a place of prayer, not a stable for animals!" The deputy smacked him, and some soldiers lashed him cruelly with their whips.

The town deputy, Picazo, thinking to find the boy cringing and frightened, was surprised to see that he was calm and tranquil. "What have you done, José?" he asked.

"I have fought like the men," responded the courageous youth.

"Don't you know that we must shoot you?" the deputy asked.

"Then shoot me," José responded. "Soon I will be next to our Lord, and I will ask Him to confound you!"

In order to terrorize him, the soldiers made him watch the hanging of one of the other *Cristeros* who had been captured. José encouraged the man, saying, "Lazaro, you will be in heaven before me. Prepare a place for me. Tell Christ the King I shall be with him soon."

He was allowed to write to his mother on Monday, February 6. In his beautiful letter he wrote: "Dearest Mother, they have taken me prisoner in combat this day. I think that very soon I am going to die, but that isn't important, Mama. I am resigned to the will of God; I die very content, because I die in the line at the side of our God. Please don't worry about my death; that is the only thing that disturbs me — that you will worry. Tell my other two brothers to follow the example of their little brother and do the will of God. Be brave and give me your blessing next to that of my father. Greetings to all of you for the last time, and you receive to the last the heart of your son that loves you so much."

Another youth was put with him. This young man was frightened, and in order to raise his spirits and keep him from denying his faith, José told him, "Come let us eat well. We will have time for all and then we will be shot. Don't worry about that. Our pain will be short, and then we will be in the sight of God." José gave the youth courage, and the boy looked up to heaven and said, "I am ready." Each day, José recited the Rosary and sang songs of faith.

On hearing that José had been captured, his father came to ask the amount to ransom him. He was told that he needed the sum of $5,000. Not having that much money, his father offered his house and some other goods, telling José's captors that if these weren't acceptable, not to kill his son until he attempted to get the money. But the deputy was going to fulfill the desire of sacrifice of this innocent one, "in the mustache of your father, with or without the money."

On February 10, after receiving the sentence of death, José wrote his last letter to one of his aunts. "My dearest Aunt, I am sentenced to death. At eight thirty will arrive the moment that I have desired. I give thanks for all the favors you have done me, you and Magdalena. I find myself incapable of writing my mother, so do me the favor of writing her and also to Maria. Tell Magdalena that even if she came to see me for the last time, I don't believe that they will let her see me or bring me Holy Communion before my death. Greetings to all, and you receive as always and for the last time the heart of your nephew, who loves you much and who desires to shed his blood in defense of the Faith. Christ lives, Christ reigns, Christ the King, and Holy Mary of Guadalupe."

About eleven o'clock that night, José was taken to the cemetery to be shot. Along the way, he continuously cried out, *"Viva Cristo Rey!"* (Long live Christ the King!) On arrival, he asked the soldiers which was to be his grave and when they pointed it out, he walked over to it to keep the enemies of Christ from laying their hands on him in order to drag him there. The *federales* asked him if he had a last message for his parents. José responded, "Tell them I will see them in heaven. *Viva Cristo Rey!*" On hearing this, one of the soldiers was angered and hit him in the head.

The commander, on seeing that the boy would not give up, ordered the soldiers to stab him with their knives so that the town would not hear the sound of gunshots. With each stab, the boy cried out, "*Viva Cristo Rey!*" Finally, the infuriated official pulled out his pistol and shot the brave young soldier in the head.

The death of the young hero caused a commotion among the Catholics of Sahuayo, and the soldiers had to guard the cemetery the following day because all wanted to come and recover some of the blood of the martyr.

José Sánchez del Río was innocent, like Saint Tarsicius, but had the strength of the martyr Saint Sebastian. The mortal remains of this child martyr rest in the Church of the Sacred Heart of Jesus in Sahuayo. His cause for beatification has been entered in Rome.

Saint David Roldán Lara
1907–1926

Twenty-five Mexican martyrs were canonized by Pope John Paul II on May 21, 2000. One of these was nineteen-year-old David Roldán, who was killed in hatred of the Faith during the turbulent years from 1915 to 1937.

He was one of the four martyrs of Zacatecas (the others were Saints Father Luis Batiz, Salvador Lara, and Manuel Moralez), who were killed under the pretext that they were trying to rouse the town against the government. Without any trial, they were executed on August 15, 1926.

David Roldán Lara was born in Chalchihuites, Zacatecas, on March 2, 1907. He was baptized later that month in the parish church.

His father, Pedro Roldán Reveles, died when David was only a year old. Widowed at a young age, his mother, Reinalda Lara Granados, was a very Christian woman who inculcated in her son a great love for Christ and His Church. She sent him to school to receive an education, and later he entered the Seminary of Durango. Because of their poor financial situation, David had to leave the seminary to help with his family's support.

Saint David Roldán Lara

A model son, David loved his mother very much and was respectful, obedient, and attentive. His friends remember him as a happy, jovial youth, orderly and responsible. Full of Christian integrity, he often helped Father Batiz, the pastor of his parish, with his pastoral duties.

At seventeen, he began to work at the El Conjuro mine near his home town. Because of his good character and responsibility, he soon became a favorite of his supervisor, the German Gustavo Windel, who named David his secretary and gave him his complete confidence. He then worked as the company's bookkeeper. David got along well with, and was held in high esteem by, his co-workers.

At work, David became acquainted with the daughter of Mr. Windel, and they became sweethearts. A little before the persecution began, he asked her to marry him.

David was a long-time member of the A.C.J.M. (Association of Young Mexican Catholics) and was elected president of the local group in 1925. He accepted the office enthusiastically. When the National League for the Defense of Religious Liberty formed a group in Chalchihuites, David was elected Vice President. Along with his friend Manual Morales and his cousin Salvador Lara, David worked hard to organize a peaceful defense of the Church by gathering signatures on a petition to overturn the oppressive anti-religious laws.

On July 29, 1926, there was a meeting of the League in Chalchihuites which was attended by over 500 people. After the meeting, the municipal president, Donaciano Pérez, and another local man falsely accused Father Batiz and his young collaborators of attempting to incite an armed rebellion. The entire town protested because everyone knew that these sturdy Catholics were only attempting to aid their persecuted church by peaceful means.

Shortly after Father Batiz was arrested, the police came and took David prisoner also. They found him at home preparing, dressed in his best clothes. David was smiling when he left with them and, on passing the home of a friend, he saluted the friend with courteous happiness. He was taken where Father Batiz and a group of other young Catholics were being held.

A group of townspeople came to try and obtain their freedom, but their efforts were in vain. Mr. Windel also came to attempt to secure their release and offered to pay a ransom to save the lives of the priest and his companions. This, too, was in vain. He was told, "Money isn't necessary. We are only going to Zacatecas with the object of taking their declarations. Nothing more will happen."

About noon, the four were put in two cars which left on the road to Zacatecas. David and his cousin Salvador left together and were put into the second car. Observers testified that they seemed very serene.

In the mountains near Puerto Santa Teresa, the cars pulled over and the prisoners were taken out. They were offered freedom if they recognized Calles' anti-religious laws. All four refused. David received absolution from Father Batiz and then witnessed the priest's heroic death.

Father Batiz and Manuel were led forward. Father Batiz asked the soldiers to free Manuel Morales because he had children to support, but Manuel told them, "I am dying for God, and God will care for my children." Then he raised his hat, and the soldiers fired, killing both.

Saint Salvador Lara

The four martyrs of Zacatecas: Father Luis Batiz,
David Roldán Lara, Salvador Lara,
and Manuel Moralez

The two youths were taken about 170 feet away from the bodies of Batiz and Morales. According to witnesses, both walked tranquilly to the indicated spot, closer to the face of the mountains, reciting an act of love. Facing their executioners, each cried out their final words: "Long live Christ the King and the Virgin of Guadalupe!"

The bullets spewed forth, ending their earthly lives. A soldier walked over to David's near-lifeless body and gave him the *tiro de gracia* in his forehead. This disfigured his face, but was not able to erase David's smile of peace and tranquility.

When the inhabitants of Chalchihuites found out what had happened, they went to collect the bodies and take them home to be waked. A little later, the families and friends were advised that General Eulogio Ortiz was on his way to take the bodies and dangle them from a tree as a warning to the other Christians. Therefore the burial had to be rushed. Near midnight, in the middle of a large rain and impending hurricane, they were taken to the municipal cemetery and given a Christian burial. ✢

32

Young Martyrs of Spain

Brothers Francisco Alfredo, Ladislao Luis, Magín Pedro,
and Raimundo Bernabé

During the bitter bloodbath of the Spanish Civil War (1936–1939), 7,937 known bishops, priests, and religious, as well as thousands of lay people, were slaughtered for the "crime" of being Catholic. Causes for many of these have been entered, and in recent years Pope John Paul II has beatified a large number of these saintly heroes and heroines of Christ the King. One hundred sixty-five Brothers of the Christian Schools died as victims of that persecution. Among these, the youngest stood as bravely as the eldest.

———

Brother Magín Pedro (Javier Salla Salto), F.S.C.
1918–1938

Javier Salla Salto was born September 3, 1918, in the province of Lerida, in the Diocese of Tarragona. He was baptized on September 8. He entered the junior novitiate for the Brothers of the Christian Schools at Cambrils in 1931, and joined the novitiate in 1934. He took the habit and received the name Magín Pedro on February 2, 1935.

Brother Magín Pedro
(Javier Salla Salto)

A scholastic, he left Cambrils with the others and went to Tarragona, where he was arrested and put in jail on the prison ship "Rio Segre." His parents were able to get him out because he was a minor.

Brother Magín was called up for military service and for some months was in the barracks, training to be a soldier. Someone in the town reported that he was a religious, and he was jailed with two of his brothers, who were noted for their own religious fervor. All three were assassinated in Juncosa on July 29, 1938. Brother Magín had not yet turned twenty.

Brother Magín Pedro is one of the group known as the Martyrs of Tarragona.

Brother Francisco Alfredo (Francisco Mallo Sánchez), F.S.C.
1916–1936

Francisco Mallo Sánchez was born August 16, 1916, and was baptized on the day of his birth. He began the junior novitiate in Fortianell in 1929 and was given the habit in 1932. Brother Francisco went to the scholasticate in Fonserannes, and in 1933 began teaching in Palamos.

When the religious persecution started in the area in July of 1936, the community of San Juan de Palamos had to disperse. Brother Hilarion Eugenio, age twenty-four, and Brother Francisco Alfredo, age nineteen, sought refuge in the house of a priest, Father Camos.

On August 12, a group of militia showed up to search the house. The militia intended to take Father Camos with them, but his mother's pleas moved them to pity and they left without him, telling the brothers to leave town as soon as possible.

Brother Francisco Alfredo
(Francisco Mallo Sánchez)

The brothers left on a bus to Palamos the following day. A man who knew them saw their departure and asked the town mayor where they were going.

The mayor replied, "To die. That way, there will be two fewer enemies!"

A group of militia went by car and intercepted the bus. They ordered the brothers to get off and then sent the bus on its way. Once off the bus, the brothers were marched about 300 meters into the forest and shot.

Some days later, a lady happened upon the bodies. She notified the torrent committee and they sent a squad to burn the bodies. The town gravedigger then interred the ashes at the spot where they were martyred. In July of 1939, some witnesses gave directions to the grave, and the ashes were exhumed and reburied in San Martin de Sasgayolas.

Brother Francisco Alfredo's cause for beatification is grouped with the brothers of the Barcelona process.

Brother Ladislao Luis (Isidro Muñoz Antolin), F.S.C.
1916–1936

Isidro Muñoz Antolin was born in Arconada on May 8, 1916. He was baptized May 14. He attended the junior novitiate and received the habit and his religious name in September of 1932. After he finished the scholasticate, he began working at Santa Cruz de Mudela in September 1935.

On July 22, 1936, a group of militia surrounded the school, overran it, and arrested the five brothers. The brothers were taken to the town's "secret police headquarters," and held for five days; then, together with two other prisoners, they were taken to another prison and held until August 19.

Their captors delighted in tormenting them. They humiliated the brothers by making them sweep the public square while they were being insulted and verbally abused. More than once, the brothers were slapped in the face and made to march military style while singing Marxist mottoes. In spite of the abuse and ridicule, the brothers showed their spirit by supporting and encouraging the other prisoners — priests and Catholic laymen. A valiant benefactress and friend of the school, Doña Cecilia Romero, brought them food and needed

Brother Ladislao Luis
(Isidro Muñoz Antolin)

items while they were held prisoner. On August 18, the brother director, Agapito León, celebrated his name day and asked permission to buy some baked goods to share with all the prisoners and the jailors. The following day, a group of militia arrived at the jail. They loaded the brothers, five priests, and twenty lay Catholics onto a truck and took them to the cemetery of Valdepanas. At midnight, the prisoners were shot and pushed into a common grave.

Brother Ladislao Luis was martyred with the brothers from Santa Cruz de Madela, and his cause for beatification is in process.

Brother Raimundo Bernabé (Ramón Altadill Cid), F.S.C.
1921–1939

Ramón Altadill Cid was born in Tortosa on Christmas Day, 1921. He was a student of the brothers and entered the junior novitiate at Cambrils at the age of twelve. He began his novitiate in 1936, but only a few days after he received the habit the brothers in formation were forced to return home.

Brother Raimundo Bernabé
(Ramón Altadill Cid)

He was still a novice when, at seventeen, he was called into the army. On January 19, while he was at the front in Tortosa, the Nationalist troops seized the city after a fierce battle and caused the Republican army to flee. More than a few of the Republican soldiers lagged behind, hoping to blend in with the enemy. Brother Raimundo was one of these and when the sergeant noticed him he demanded to know what Raimundo was doing.

"I can't take any more, Sergeant. I am so tired that I cannot move," Raimundo replied. After a few more exchanges, Brother Raimundo confided, "You know, it's just that I am a religious..."

The sergeant refused to hear any more; he took his bayonet and pierced the young man saying "Die, you swine!"

Brother Raimundo's body remained on the battlefield with the corpses of many others that fell that day. Because of a lack of documentation, there is no cause for beatification for this young brother. ✚

33

Young Martyrs of Thailand
Blesseds Bibiana Khamphai, Cecilia Butsi, and Maria Phon

During the turbulent years of the 1940s, the situation in much of Europe and Asia was unsettled. In this tense atmosphere, the normally tolerant Thailand began a religious persecution. No religious or cultural pluralism would be tolerated, and Catholicism was considered a foreign religion, although it had existed in the country for over three hundred years.

The parish priest of Songkhon, a Catholic village of rice farmers on the Maekhong River, was banished and deported. Armed policemen went door to door intimidating the people, ordering them to abandon their faith in Christ. Although the people were frightened, they remained quietly steadfast.

In the absence of the priest, the valiant lay catechist Philip Siphong and two Sisters of the Congregation of the Lovers of the Holy Cross, Sisters Agnes and Lucia, continued to catechize and encourage the people. On December 16, 1940, the catechist was taken into the woods and shot.

In spite of their grief and fear, the sisters continued their work, teaching the children of the village and encouraging the faithful. The police continued to keep up the pressure on the community, firing their rifles in the air and shouting threats.

On Christmas day, Mr. Lue, the police officer in charge of Songkhon, came to the convent and found the sisters teaching catechism. Furious, he berated the sisters, telling them, "I've told you many times not to speak about Jesus. You must not mention God in Thailand, otherwise I'll kill you all."

Sister Agnes, the superior, became indignant and asked him, "Mr. Policeman, do you mean to say that you will kill us all because we are Catholics and loyal to our Catholic Faith. Do you really mean that, Mr. Policeman?"

Mr. Lue confirmed his threat and Sister Agnes said, "Be sure you have sufficient guns and bullets."

"Oh yes, we have enough guns and bullets to kill all of you." Mr. Lue retorted.

"Then be sure you polish the barrels of your guns lest the bullets get stuck," the brave sister retorted.

Blessed Bibiana Khamphai
1925–1940

Blessed Cecilia Butsi
1924–1940

Blessed Maria Phon
1926–1940

Cecilia Butsi was one of the helpers in the kitchen of the mission. At a meeting which took place in front of the Church later that day, she stood up to affirm that she was a Christian, in spite of the threat of death made by the police.

That night the sisters prepared themselves and their companions for their coming martyrdom by prayers and hymns, singing throughout the night. Cecilia was with them, along with their cook, Agatha Phutta, and two other aides of the mission, Bibiana Khamphai and Maria Phon. Bibiana was a girl of blameless life who used to come to the mission. Maria Phon lived with her aunt and was assiduous in assisting at Mass and receiving the Sacraments. She came to the mission for instruction and was a gentle and well-behaved adolescent.

Blessed Bibiana Khamphai

Also with them were two other young girls, Suwan and Sorn.

Late that same night, Sister Agnes wrote a letter to the police. This letter is a simple yet moving and powerful profession of a lively faith.

This letter is preserved in the diocesan archives as a precious relic. In part, it reads:

"To the Chief of Police in Songkhon. Yesterday evening you received your order ... to wipe out, definitely, the name of God, the only Lord of our lives and minds. We adore Him only, sir. ... We do profess that the religion of Christ is the only true religion. Therefore, we would like to give our answer to your question, asked yesterday evening ... which we did not have a chance to respond (to) because we were unprepared for it. ... Please carry out your order. We are ready to give back our lives to God who has given them to us. ... Please open the door of heaven to us so that we can confirm that outside the religion of Christ no one can go to heaven. ... We are well prepared. When we will be gone we will remember you. Please take pity on our souls. We will be thankful to you and will be grateful to you for it. And on the last day we will see each other face to face. ... We wish to be witnesses to You, dear God. ... We have already made up our minds, dear Sir."

The following afternoon, the police arrived at the convent and shouted, "Are you ready, Sisters? If you are, go straight to the bank of the Maekhong."

Sister Agnes objected, "No, that is not the place for us to die for Christ. We must go to the cemetery, the holy place."

Blessed Cecilia Butsi

As the sisters and the children walked in line to the cemetery, they were singing hymns and calling out to the people, "Good-bye, we are going to heaven, we are going to become martyrs for Christ."

Realizing that the group was to be killed, the townspeople began to follow the brave sisters and their companions. When Suwan's father realized what was happening, he rushed to rescue his daughter. She clung to Sister Agnes, begging "Mother Agnes, help me please, I want to die with you and go to heaven." Her father snatched her away, carried her home and locked her in a room to prevent her joining the others.

At the cemetery, the brave group knelt down beside a fallen tree trunk and continued praying and singing. Sister Agnes turned and addressed the police: "You may kill us but you cannot kill the Church and you cannot kill God. One day the Church will return to Thailand and will flourish more than ever. You will see with your own eyes that what I am now saying will come true. So we thank you from our hearts for killing us and sending us to heaven. From there we will pray for you." Then, turning to her companions, Sister Agnes said, "My dear friends we will soon be in heaven." She continued, "Mr. Policeman, we are ready, please do your duty."

Immediately the police discharged a volley and left the cemetery, shouting to the people. "Bury them like dogs, for they are bad people." The poor villagers, who were watching the scene from behind nearby bushes, rushed forward and found that both Sister Agnes and Phon were still alive although badly wounded.

Blessed Maria Phon

Looking around, Phon asked, "Where is heaven?"

Sister Agnes, on her part, asked "Where are the police?" On being told that they had left, she said, "Then you better call them back, I'm not dead yet."

One of the villagers returned to the village to inform the police that Sister Agnes and Phon, although badly wounded, were still alive.

Sorn, who was at the end of the line, stood up, looked around and exclaimed "Where is heaven?" Although her clothes were splattered with blood, when the villagers asked if she was hurt she replied, "I'm afraid not. I don't feel any pain."

She was advised to run away, as the police were coming back. Today, Sorn still lives in Songkhon and is a catechist.

Shortly after, the police returned to the cemetery and killed the wounded Agnes and Phon.

———

The villagers buried the six holy martyrs hurriedly, placing two bodies in each grave; they did not have time to make coffins. Today, the relics of the seven Blessed Martyrs of Thailand rest in beautiful glass reliquaries behind the altar of the Shrine of Our Lady of the Martyrs of Thailand in Songkhon.

A number of eyewitnesses, including some of those who took part in the burial of the martyrs, are still alive. They are proud to recall the bravery, the loyalty to Christ, and the wonderful faith displayed on that momentous day, December 26, 1940, by the Holy Martyrs of Songkhon.

The persecution of the Christians went on for another four years and then religious freedom returned to Thailand. At that time, the local Ordinary began setting up the canonical investigations on the case of these seven brave servants of God. They were beatified October 22, 1989, by Pope John Paul II. ✧

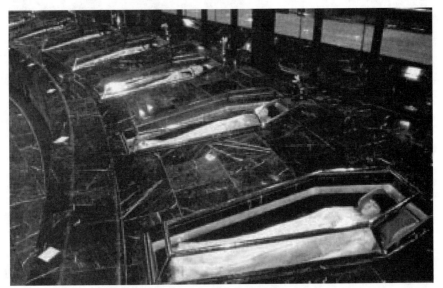

Tombs of the Holy Thai Martyrs

34

Young Martyrs of Uganda

Saints Achilles Kiwanuka, Ambrose Kibuka, Anatole Kiriggwajjo,
Athanasius Bazekuketta, Denis Ssebuggwawo, Gyavira, Kizito,
Mugagga, Mbaga Tuzinde,
and Mukasa Kiriwawanvu
Circa 1865–1887

Never in the history of the Church has a group of Christians lived, suffered, and died in so close an imitation of the Apostles and early Roman martyrs as have the martyrs of Uganda. Ten of these twenty-two heroic martyrs were age twenty or younger. In spite of their youth, they were not afraid to die for Christ, and the fountain of blood shed by them has watered the seed of the Catholic faith in Africa.

In July of 1885, the Society of Missionaries of Africa, commonly known as the White Fathers, was invited to return to the Kingdom of Buganda (now part of the nation of Uganda). They had begun their work in the country in 1879, the first Catholic missionaries to enter the deep interior of the African continent. Pope Leo XIII had assigned them an enormous new mission territory in the

Saint Charles Lwanga baptized Kizito, Gyavira, Mugagga, and Mbaga Tuzinde the night before their death

heart of Africa. They entered the Kingdom of Buganda, bearing before them the standard of the Sacred Heart instead of any political flag.

Within a few years, the fathers had mastered the language, Luganda, so well that they wrote a grammar of it, and the first book ever to be printed in the language was a catechism composed by the Fathers. They

Kizito

began giving instructions and making converts. In 1882, however, because of rumors of assassination plots against the missionaries and the erratic whims of King Mutesa, the missionaries withdrew from the area. After the king's death in 1884, his son Mwanga, who had been a friend of the missionaries, sent canoes to bring them back. He gave the missionaries a new site for a mission.

The happiest news was that the small group of converts they had left had spent their time instructing others in the Faith. Apostles in the true sense of the word, they prayed and read their catechism daily, then taught their relatives, friends, and servants. They lived as Christians, although the prevalent pagan religion was an animistic spirit-worship in which polygamy, slavery, pillage, and massacre in war, drunkenness and many forms of debauchery were acceptable. The Christians remained faithful to a single wife, did much of their own work themselves rather than delegating it to servants or slaves, and refused to indulge in excesses. They were peaceful, remaining loyal to the king in all things that did not conflict with God's law. They continued their regular jobs while carrying out many Christian acts of mercy.

During the three-year absence of the missionaries, a plague struck the country; the Christians valiantly went out and nursed the sick with no thought for themselves. John Mary Muzeyi reported that during the epidemic, the Christians had baptized all the Christian catechumens who died. The Fathers were happy to see that during their absence the Christian community had grown from a small handful to several hundred, including many in the king's court and the surrounding area. These came for baptism as soon as the priests came back.

Shortly after he ascended the throne, Mwanga became convinced of his absolute power, and began to reign as despotically as had his father. Much of his power was based on his subjects' fear. Because the peaceful Christians did not seem afraid of him, he began to worry about his retention of power should his country become Christian. In addition, the king's top advisor, some of the chiefs, the queen mother, and the witch doctors all feared and hated the Christians, and they attempted to influence the king against them.

In the king's court, as his personal servants, there were about four hundred royal pages, chosen from among the best youth in the country. In order to preserve their purity, the Christians among the pages refused to indulge in despotic excesses with the king, and it was over them that the major storm of persecution broke out.

In November of 1885, the Anglican missionaries announced that Bishop James Hannington, the first Anglican bishop of East Equatorial Africa, and six other missionaries planned to enter the country in an attempt to open a short route to the Lake Victoria area. The Anglicans were particularly feared because they were English, and the king gave the order for their massacre. Joseph Mukasa Balikuddembe, who was the king's majordomo as well as one of the leading catechists for the Christians, courageously spoke up and asked the king just to forbid them entry, but the king would not change his mind, and the Anglicans were killed. At this point, the king and his advisors began to think of getting rid of Joseph.

In addition to being the leader of the Catholic Christians, Joseph, in his position as majordomo, had carefully watched over the young Christian pages. When the king sent for one of them, Joseph would hide him, or send him out of the way, knowing that he was placing himself in great danger. Finally, the king found an excuse to get rid of the troublesome Joseph. The king felt ill, and Joseph gave him an opium pill, a customary medicine. However, the king stated that it was an attempt to poison him, and gave the order for Joseph to be burned alive. Out of pity, the executioner had Joseph beheaded before burning his body. The brave catechist

Athanasius Bazekuketta

sent a message of forgiveness to the king, and called for his repentance.

Charles Lwanga and several of the other catechumens working in the court realized that they, too, would probably be executed, so they went to the mission for Baptism. Realizing the danger of the Christians in the court, the missionaries were hesitant about sending them back. Smiling, the newly baptized group asked them, "Is it bad to go to heaven?"

Although the king announced that he planned to kill all "those who pray," the Christians remained resolute. Charles Lwanga took Joseph's place, and he, too, guarded the purity of the Christian pages by hiding them. The missionaries spent their time preparing the Christians for death and comforting them.

King Mwanga had been greatly frightened by Joseph's last words in which the catechist said that if he didn't repent he would accuse him before the court of God. There was a shower of shooting stars twelve days after Joseph's death, a number of fires in the compound, and lightning struck one of the huts. To the king's superstitious mind, these seemed signs that Joseph had cursed him. Near Easter, the priests received word that a plan to massacre all the Christians was

Athanasius Bazekuketta

underway, and they sent word for them not to come to the mission, hoping to avoid further conflict.

In order to get his sister, Clara Nalumansi, out of the way, the king assigned her to guard the royal tombs. A Christian, she burned the fetishes at the tombs and sent away the witch doctors. This made her brother furious, but he was afraid to have her executed. Returning unexpectedly from an unsuccessful hunt, the frustrated king found all the Christian pages missing. When one of them returned, he confessed that he had been with Denis Ssebuggwawo, who had been teaching him a religion lesson. Furiously, the king called for sixteen-year-old Denis and thrust a lance into his body. Later, he commanded the boy to be taken away and finished off.

The pagan pages advised all the Christians to flee, but the Christian pages refused. Since they were in the king's personal service, an attempt to hide would have been seen as a revolt. Although several of the youngest did hide for a brief time they soon returned, and all the Christian pages prepared to die for their religion.

The king shut the gates of the compound, called all the chiefs and executioners, and had the drums beaten all night. Under the direction of Charles Lwanga, all the Christian pages assembled and spent the night in prayer. The youngest page, Kizito, had been begging for Baptism, but his request had been denied up until this time because the Fathers felt he had not studied the Faith long enough. Charles baptized him and four others, although the Christian names they received are not known. He then encouraged the entire group to confess their Faith boldly and to continue to pray. He comforted little Kizito by telling him that if they were sentenced to death, he would hold his hand, and

The death of Athanasius Bazekuketta

together they would die for Christ. Only fourteen or fifteen, Kizito was greatly loved for his tremendous gaiety. He was a good sportsman and an outstanding swimmer and wrestler.

When all the chiefs and executioners were assembled, the order was given for the pages to appear. Then the king issued a single sharp order: "Let all those who pray go over there." Taking Kizito's hand, Charles Lwanga stood up and walked to the spot indicated. The others followed his lead, including the Anglicans; one witness later reported that their faces were a picture of joy.

Bruno Serunkuma, one of the king's bodyguards, silently left his place and joined the pages. Mugagga, a page who was about sixteen, joined the group. Other than the Christians, no one had known he had secretly been taking instructions at night. Mugagga was remarkable among the pages for his joyfulness and readiness to help. As often as he was tempted by the king to offend chastity and deny his Faith, he refused energetically. When others, not knowing he had been baptized a few hours before by Charles Lwanga, were surprised to see him, he replied, "Have we too not also offered ourselves to Jesus Christ?"

The cousins Achilles Kiwanuka and Ambrose Kibuka burned their amulets

The adopted son of the chief executioner, Mbaga Tuzinde, was a part of the group. He was loyal and a model of perseverance. His father ordered him to hide, and when the seventeen-year-old boy did not move, one of the other executioners told him to obey his father. He answered, "My Father whom I must obey is in heaven." His father begged him to deny his Faith, and Mbaga answered bravely, "I want to die for the cause of God," as he pointed to heaven.

During the ritual sentencing, Father Lourdel had been waiting outside the gate where he was prevented by the guards from entering. As the bound prisoners left, he watched them walk by. He noticed that Kizito was laughing as if it were a game. He blessed them for the last time, and then went to the king to plead for their lives. Finally, he begged, "At least send me where you have sent my children," but the king refused. Several others who had been imprisoned for different reasons joined the death march, preceded by the chief executioner, beating his drum. The group, which included about thirty Anglican and Catholic Christians, was marched to a site at Namugongo, about sixteen miles from the king's compound, where a large pyre of wood could be built on top of a hill.

A number of the martyrs were killed along the way. When the group passed the village of Andrew Kaggwa, the chief musician for the king, the king's advisor demanded that Andrew be executed. Andrew had been expecting this, and had sent his family to safety. He was praying in his hut when he was dragged out to the group. His arm was cut off with a knife, and then he was beheaded and dismembered. Pontian Ngondwe was stabbed to death near Mengo. Gonzaga Gonza was speared to death, and his body was thrown on an ant hill.

The death of Saint Matthias Mulumba was the cruelest. Accused by the prime minister of doing his own cooking, Matthias smilingly replied, "Am I on trial for my thinness or my religion?" In a rage, the prime minister ordered that Matthias be made to suffer more than the others, and taunted him by asking, "Will your God save you?" Matthias quietly replied, "He will rescue my soul, but you will not see." His arms and legs were hacked off, and pieces of his flesh were burned in front of him. To prolong his death agony, his arteries and veins were tied off, and he was left, mutilated, to die in the broiling sun. Two days later, some slaves coming to cut reeds heard him cry out for water, but ran off, terrified, because of the rule that anyone helping a condemned man was made to share the same punishment.

Anatole Kiriggwajjo

By custom, at each crossroad the executioners would kill a prisoner to frighten passers-by. Near Kampala, Athanasius Bazekuketta, age twenty, volunteered. He was beheaded and dismembered on May 27. Serene and calm, Athanasius had been loved and respected by everyone at court, and after his death the others encouraged each other by recalling his courage.

At the village of Mityana, the leading catechist, Noah Mawaggali, had sent all the Christians into hiding, though he himself refused to leave. He was speared and tied to a tree where he was cut to make the blood flow in order to attract wild dogs. He died after several hours of agony. Matilda Munaku, Noah's sister, courageously gave herself up to the executioners, but she was simply imprisoned. Noah's wife was taken before the prime minister and cruelly beaten.

When the group reached Namugongo, the prisoners were left bound, and were thrown into huts to await execution. Many of the details of their martyrdom came from Denis Kamyuka, a fifteen-year-old page whose life was spared. He testified that the older ones encouraged the younger men. They prayed constantly, and even the very youngest member of the group, Kizito, did not seem sad or worried. Kizito told one of his companions, "Say the Our Father and suffer bravely."

In addition to the Catholics and Anglicans, there were seven or eight non-Christians who were in prison. The Christians began to instruct them, and all but two began praying with the Christians. The next morning, two of the Anglicans spoke with the executioners, telling them it was not right to burn those who did not pray, so the pagan page Aliwali and the Moslem Adudala were taken back safely.

Achilles Kiwanuka

From this time on, the group was unanimous in constant prayer, and no one testified to a single lament.

The prisoners were kept for several days and then lined up to be marched to the pyre. One of the executioners passed down the line with a long reed lighted at the tip, tapping the head of each prisoner in a pagan ritual to prevent the spirits of the condemned from returning to bother the king. If a prisoner failed to receive the tap, he knew he was reprieved. Reaching Charles Lwanga, the executioner said, "This one's for me," indicating that his suffering would be greater. Calmly, the young man told the others, "My friends, good-bye. We'll meet again in heaven." He was tied to a low stake and burned. Although his eyes blinked incessantly with the pain, Charles continued to pray, and thought first of his executioner's soul. Quietly, he told Senkole, "How happy I should be if you,

too, were to embrace my religion."
Although Senkole simply snickered,
he later became a catechumen.

At the execution platform, the
executioners, dressed in animal
skins with their faces painted with
red paint and soot, began chanting
in order to frighten the prisoners.
Their cruel chant, translated, was
"Today, the parents of these children are going to weep." Neither
the sight of the platform or of the
executioners apparently frightened
any of the group. The prisoners
were rolled in reed mats and tightly
bound, and three of the reprieved
pages were set aside. Saint Bruno
sadly told these three, "It would
have been better for us all to die

Ambrose Kibuka and Achilles Kiwanuka

together. The king will make you give up religion, my children."
These three protested, asking to be executed with the others, but they
were ignored.

One of the martyrs called out to Denis Kamyuka, "Tell Mapera
[the native name for Father Lourdel] that we have been faithful!"

Mbaga Tuzinde, the adopted son of the chief executioner, had
been kept separate from the others in a final attempt to persuade him
to recant. The executioner had his son unbound and made him kneel
before him, as the heartbroken father made a final appeal. The young
man bravely refused, so his father ordered his neck to be broken with
a club before he was put on the fire. Two of the Anglicans were also
accorded the same privilege.

At sixteen, Mukasa Kiriwawanvu had a light heart and was, in a
way, the court jester. He was still a catechumen when condemned to
death — although he had not been baptized by water, he was baptized
by blood. Before dying, he cried lightheartedly to the other martyrs,
"I am happy to find you. I was afraid they might have left me aside
and forgotten me in prison."

Gyavira, age seventeen, was a model of purity which he always defended energetically in the midst of the corrupt court. He and Mukasa Kiriwawanvu were friends, but one day they had a quarrel and Mukasa beat Gyavira with a stick. As a result, Mukasa was put in prison. When Gyavira saw his old friend on the road to martyrdom, be said, "Mukasa, my friend, how happy I am to see you again. I thank God for this reunion. Let us die together for Jesus Christ." They shook hands as a token of forgiveness and were burned together.

Achilles Kiwanuka, age eighteen, used to say, "As for me, they may kill me, but I shall never turn away from my religion." Along with Ambrose, he burned the pagan fetish given to him by his parents when he went to court. He sometimes sneaked out at night to go to the mission to receive Communion. When he realized that his martyrdom was coming, he went to say good-bye to his pagan parents, remaining steadfast in spite of their heartbroken entreaties for him to abandon his faith and save himself.

Mugagga

Anatole Kiriggwajjo, age twenty, because of his gentle ways and mild temperament, was one of the favorite pages of both Kings Mutesa and Mwanga. He was a model of humility. Anatole turned down a very advantageous position so as not to be exposed to the danger of sin. King Mwanga remarked, "These Christians do not want even the honors I am offering them." When others spoke of the great honor the post conferred, Anatole merely answered, "God is greater." While waiting to be burned, he encouraged his companions by saying, "Our friends who have been killed are already with God. Let us stand fast like them and we, too, shall join them in heaven."

At eighteen, Ambrose Kibuka was at once a faithful servant of the king and a fearless confessor of the Faith. He was the inseparable companion of his cousin Achilles Kiwanuka. He had burnt the fetish given to him by his father as soon as he understood how useless the pagan charm was.

Denis Ssebuggwawo

With burning torches, the platform was set afire on June 3, 1886. Denis Kamyuka remembered hearing an intense murmur, the prayers of the dying invoking God. Saint Bruno called out, "You kill the body only; the soul belongs to God," and then resumed his praying. Young Mugagga called out to a companion "Good-bye, my friend, I am going away to the good God."

On the way back, one of the executioners said, "We have killed many men, but never such as these. The others did nothing but moan and weep, but these prayed right to the end."

With pain and with pride, the White Fathers learned the news of the heroic deaths of the martyrs. The faithfulness of the other Christians, who nightly came to the mission for the Sacraments, consoled them. Because of the martyrs' example, the Christians were so unafraid of the persecutions that the Fathers had a difficult time persuading them not to give themselves up for execution. The priests counseled them to return to their villages and become true apostles by teaching others about the true religion.

Pope Paul VI canonized the 22 Martyrs of Uganda in 1964. ✣

35

Young Martyrs of Vietnam

*Blessed Anre Phu Yen and Saints Andrew Trong Van Tram, Giuse Tuuc,
and Thomas Thien Tran (Dien)*

In 1988, Pope John Paul II canonized a group of 117 martyrs
who suffered and died for the faith in the region we now know as
Vietnam. Ninety-six of the martyrs were Vietnamese, 11 were
Spaniards, and 10 were French; 58 members of the group were associated with the Paris Foreign Mission Society, and 59 were members
of the Dominican family. All were martyred at different times and
places during the eighteenth and nineteenth centuries.

Untold thousands suffered and died to bring the message of
Christ, have it take root, and bear fruit on Vietnamese soil. From the
outset, Christianity in Indochina came under official disfavor, and in
1553 an imperial edict forbad the "false doctrine of Jesus" being
preached by a certain Ignatius. The history of Christian martyrdom
in Vietnam runs concurrent with four centuries of recorded Church
history in the area.

Christianity was brought to Vietnam in 1627 by the Jesuit Father
Alexander Rhodes. He began his work in Tonkin, in the northern part
of the country. Later in the same century, Dominican missionaries
accompanied Portuguese exploration and mercantile ventures into the
Indian Ocean. After failing to evangelize Buddhist Cambodia, these
Portuguese Dominicans went to Vietnam, where they were better
received by a population where the majority had no formal religion
other than that of ancestor-worship. By the end of the 17th Century,
Spanish Dominicans from Manila were also working in Vietnam.

During the first centuries, aliens were not allowed permanent residence, so efforts at evangelization came and went, as did the missionaries. In the 17th Century, tolerant reigning dynasties allowed
more fruitful work on the part of Jesuit missionaries. These Jesuits
arrived in the region after the Japanese ruler forced them out in an
attempt to eradicate the Christian faith from his empire. During the
second half of that century, a second group of missionaries came from

the Paris Foreign Mission Society, which was founded in 1659 to spread the Gospel in Southeast Asia.

The political organization of Vietnam was much like China's: an empire ruled by dynasties that succeeded each other. Local viceroys and mandarins assisted the emperor, who was considered the "son of heaven," and was an absolute ruler.

In 1711, Emperor An Vuong issued the first Edict of Persecution of Christians. Many Christians lost their lives in 1745 and again in 1773. In 1798, the Virgin Mary appeared in the mountain jungle near LaVang to bring a message of motherly love to her Vietnamese persecuted children.

Under the reign of Gia Long, from 1802-1820, Christianity was officially accepted and grew rapidly. By 1820, there were an estimated 400,000 Vietnamese Catholics, in three apostolic vicariates. The special development of catechists was characteristic of the Vietnamese Dominican Mission. They lived in community in houses called Houses of God, and were dedicated to evangelization under the authority of the apostolic vicars. Women were organized and called sisters, and were consecrated to works of charity. Lay Dominicans and

The young Vietnamese martyrs were among this
group of 117 martyrs canonized in 1988

members of the Confraternity of the Rosary were numerous and of great help to the missionaries. A large infrastructure of social works began to be created in Vietnam.

After this brief time of peace, persecution again mounted and reached unparalleled heights during the reigns of emperors Minh Manh, Thieu Tri, and Tu Duc (1830-1864). This time period is known as the "era of the martyrs" — thousands were slain. After 1832, the Annamite King Minh Manh excluded all foreign missionaries and required native Christians to apostatize by trampling on the cross.

The tortures inflicted on the martyrs are beyond imagination. One particular type was the wearing of a *cangue*, two planks tied with chains, one on the shoulders and one on the feet. Christians were beheaded, burned, strangled, whipped, exposed to raw weather, crucified, stomped on by elephants, and starved. Pliers were used to tear the flesh away bit by bit. Christians were placed in cages like animals, and some were continuously beaten with sticks.

A decree promulgated in 1854 by Emperor Tu Duc was meant to eradicate the Christian religion from his dominions. Between the years 1856 and 1862, thousands of Christians died. In the province of Nam-dinh alone there were more than 30,000 martyred. In the fifty years before the establishment of the French Protectorate in 1883, an estimated 300,000 Christians suffered death or extreme hardship as their homes and villages were destroyed. It was possible to gather clear information on only 1,700 of them; for some, even the year of their death is unknown. By 1917, the causes for canonization of 1,315 were introduced. Representative groups of clergy and laity, both native and foreign, have been beatified at various times since 1900.

Catholic Vietnamese communities thrive where the Vietnamese have immigrated to other parts of the world. Although the Church in Vietnam is still repressed by the Vietnamese government, by all accounts it is a strong one and growing.

Blessed Anre Phu Yen
1625–1644

Blessed Anre, only 19 years old, is considered the proto-martyr of the Church in Vietnam. Born in the province of Phuù Yeân in 1625, Anre was baptized at the age of 15, along with his widowed mother and his siblings, by Father Alexander Rhodes. A year later, Anre joined a group of twelve catechists who assisted the missionaries.

Death of Blessed Anre Phu Yen

The authorities had decided to arrest and execute the leader of the missionaries, Father Ignatius, but when the soldiers came for him, he was away. Anre offered himself in place of Ignatius. He was arrested and led to the head official, who questioned him about his faith. Courageously, knowing the consequences, he said, "I wish I had a thousand lives to offer to God in thanksgiving for what He has done for me." Another Christian, named Andrew, was in jail with him. Both were condemned to death for being Christians.

Father Rhodes mobilized all of the Portuguese of Hoi An to intercede in their favor. His cell mate, Andrew, was pardoned because he had children, but the mandarin said of Anre Phu Yen, "This one has to die so all will know how to obey the Lord [Lord Nguyen of Hué]."

Anre calmly and joyously awaited the day of execution, asking his loved ones to pray that he might remain faithful to the end. Stabbed repeatedly, he constantly invoked the name of Jesus. The morning of July 26, 1644, Anre was taken to a court of justice in GoXu to be executed. The soldiers attempted to prevent Father Rhodes from approaching the kneeling martyr, but the captain allowed him to approach. Anre was beheaded. Rhodes took the blessed martyr's body to Macao and the head to Rome.

Saint Andrew Trong Van Tram
1817–1835

Andrew was raised in a devout Catholic family of Hué. He often aided the missionaries of the Paris Foreign Mission Society who were working in the area. His mother was a weaver and taught her skills to her son. Although she considered getting a wife for him, he turned the offer down and enlisted in the royal weaver's platoon for a military career.

After a French attack on Nao Naung, Emperor Minh Maing ordered a census on Catholic soldiers, suspecting that some of them may have aided the enemy. In November 1834, Andrew was arrested with seven companions. Tortured repeatedly, Andrew remained firm. "If you have pity on me, then I am lucky. I will do whatever you want, but never will I step over the cross to reject my faith."

While he was being held in the Citadel Prison, Andrew's mother visited him daily and encouraged him in his faith. Later, he calmly related how the prison officials had tried to use his love for his mother to tempt him to apostatize: "They kept telling me that I am sinning against loyalty both toward the king and my mother, and questioning me on the whereabouts of paradise. I replied to them that they should mind their own business and I knew well what loyalty means to me."

In prison, Andrew remained joyful and amiable, constantly trying to lift the spirits of the other inmates. Daily, he led them in the Rosary. He shared his food with others who were near starvation. Seeing Andrew's goodness, the guards allowed him to go out at night to attend to his affairs. Twice, he was able to go to Confession and Communion and to visit his mother.

Before his execution, his cousin visited him in prison and Andrew told him, "Stay with my mother as an apprentice for the weaver's trade, and to assist her. Please tell her that I am greatly blessed to die for the Lord and I hope she will take care of herself physically and religiously. As for me, everything has been accomplished; nothing can disturb me any more."

Andrew was taken to the execution field on a rainy, windy November 28, 1835. Witnesses testified that his face was joyful as he walked beside the executioner. He was holding his Rosary in his hand. Hearing the news, his mother ran to see her son for the last time. They exchanged final farewells, and she asked him if he owed any debts so she could repay them.

At the field, the executioners removed his yoke and chains, and Andrew asked them to give the chains to his mother.

The drums rolled, the sword fell, and the courageous young man was beheaded. Andrew's courageous mother, after paying a fee, took up her son's severed head. She paid an additional fee to recover his body. Returning home, she sent a messenger to bring a priest who was hiding in the mountains to say the funeral Mass, asking him to wear red vestments because "today is a day of joy for the family," the triumphant day of a martyr. (In Vietnam, red is a happy, joyful color worn on festive occasions.)

In the beatification decree, Pope Leo XIII pointed out, "Among the Vietnamese martyrs there is Andrew Trong, who is famous not only because of his own courage, but also because of his mother's heroism, since she imitated our Blessed Mother in sharing sufferings with her son, standing near him, witnessing his death, and after the decapitation, embracing her son's head."

Saint Giuse Tuuc
1852–1862

This young saint was decapitated at the age of ten. Little else is known about him.

Saint Thomas Thien Tran (Dien)
1820–1838

Thomas was a seminarian who studied with the Paris Foreign Mission Society and was preparing to be ordained when he was arrested in 1838.

Thomas was born in 1820 to a devout Catholic family in the province of Quaung Binh. He had two older sisters, one of whom became a nun. His father died when Thomas was only ten years old, so the priest, Father Chinh, helped him with the education he would need to become a seminarian. His aunt was the superior of a convent, and she too encouraged him in a religious vocation.

At 18, Thomas was summoned to enter An Ninh Seminary in Di Loan. Emperor Kinh Maing had begun a severe persecution of the Catholics in order to eradicate the religion from Vietnam. In spite of the danger, Thomas resolutely set off for Di Loan, accompanied by his sister Saoo. Their sister Yean sent a warning to her siblings, telling them that the rector of the seminary, Father Kim, had gone underground. Thomas replied, "Although I may not see him, I must get there to be sure. He has called me. I cannot help but report."

Thomas was caught and arrested on the way to Di Loan. He was bound with a yoke and taken to Quaung Tro. After being tortured and beaten, he was offered his freedom if he gave up his religion. The brave young man answered, "The religion that teaches me to worship God is the real one; I cannot forsake it. I prefer being beheaded to rejecting my religion."

Seeing how stalwart the handsome young Catholic boy was, the mandarin then attempted to tempt him into rejecting the faith. He offered to marry Thomas to his daughter and make him a government officer, a high position that would give him wealth and power. Thomas remained steadfast, declaring, "I only wish to become an officer in heaven rather than an officer on this earth."

In sympathy, the mandarin tried to encourage Thomas to step over the cross as the royal order mandated and told him he would then allow him to go home and practice his faith however he wished. Thomas would not give in, even by faking a denial of the true faith. His attitude angered the mandarin, who had Thomas and a priest, Father Phan, beaten and left in the burning sun with no food or water. Afterwards, Thomas was tortured with white hot pincers that burned his flesh. Yet he did not cease to pray that God give him strength to endure and remain loyal. Finally he was sentenced to death. He was strangled on September 21, 1838, at the execution field of Nhan Bieau. ✣

SELECTED BIBLIOGRAPHY

A Benedictine Nun of Stanbrook. *Anne: The Life of Venerable Anne de Guigné, 1911-1922*. Rockford, Illinois: TAN Books, 1997.

Alonso, O.M. Sr. M. Teresa de Jesus. *Sonia: Una Muchacha Que Ha Dejado Huella*. Barcelona: Contemplativas Minimas: 1991

Ball, Ann. *Modern Saints: Their Lives and Faces*. Rockford, Illinois: TAN Books and Publishers, 1983.

Ball, Ann. *Modern Saints: Their Lives and Faces*. Rockford, Illinois: TAN Books and Publishers, 1988.

Bednarczyk, Piotr and Bialobok, Jan. *Carolina Kózka; il Coraggio dell' Innocenza*. Rome: Citta Nuova, 1987.

Bertoglio, M. Guadalupe Lucia. *Mari Carmen: La Fuerza del Perdon*. Madrid: Ediciones Palabra, 1999.

Bialobok, P. Bednarczyk. *Carolina Kózka*. Rome: Città Nuova Editrice, 1987.

Biancho, Enzo and Maraldi, Assunata. *First Centenary of Don Bosco's Missions*. Rome: SDB Publishers, 1975.

Boday, Jeno, S.J. Graham, Aloysius, S.J., trans. *Stephen Kaszap Servant of God*. The Company of Jesus, undated.

Bossa, Barry. *A Passionist with Promise*. Marytown: Immaculata Magazine, September 1981.

Bunson, Matthew, Margaret, and Stephen. *John Paul II's Book of Saints*. Huntington, Indiana: Our Sunday Visitor, 1999.

Cejas, José Miguel. *Montse Grases*. Madrid: Ediciones Rialp, S.A., 1994.

Clark, Francis X., S.J. *Asian Saints*. Quezon City, Philippines: Claretian Publications, 2000.

Conferencia del Episcopado Mexicano. *Viva Cristo Rey*. Mexico D.F.: Gema, 1991.

Cruz, Joan Carroll. *Secular Saints*. Rockford, Illinois: TAN Books.

Deister, John L. *Martires Mexicanos*. 1928.

Dolci, Maria Paola, trans. Montonati, Angelo. "Maria Orsola, A Sixteen-year-old Girl Who Discovers that God is Love," *The Champions.* Torino: Elle Di Ci, 1997.

Evangelist, Sister M., O.P. *Mission Fulfilled.* New York: Dell Publishing Co., 1961.

George, Susan. *Danny's Life, Suffering, and Death: A Mystery in Christ and Trinitarian Life.* Santa Rosa Beach, Florida: SOLT, 1999.

Havers, Guillermo, *Testigos de Cristo en Jalisco.* Guadalajara, Ediciones Promesa, 1988.

Kim, Rev. Joseph Chang-mun and Chung, John Jae-sun. *Catholic Korea.* Seoul: Saint Joesph Publishing Company, 1984.

Kim, Rev. Chang-seok Thaddeus. *Lives of 103 Martyr Saints of Korea.* Seoul: Catholic Publishing House, 1984.

Lopez de Uralde, Maria Luisa, Ca. Ch. *Teresita's Story.* Madrid: Carmelite Sisters of Charity, 1993.

Madden, Daniel. *A Greater Love.* New Rochelle, New York: Salesian Missions, 1999.

Madigan, Leo. *Princesses of the Kingdom.* Cork: Kolbe Publications, 2001.

Marion, Francis. *New African Saints: The Twenty-two Martyrs of Uganda.* Milan: Ancora Publishers, 1964.

McBrearty, Neil, C.P. *The Boy Who Knew What He Wanted.* Dublin: M.H. Gill and Son Ltd., 1957.

Menegazzo, P. Federico, C.P. *Il Venerable Galileo Nicolini.* Rome: Postulazione Generale Padri Passionisti, 1982.

Mirra, Pierluigi. *Gromoaldo Santamaria, Studente Passionista.* Napoli: Editrice Pasquarelli, 1994.

Nguyen, Rev. Vinh Quang. "The Vietnamese Catholic Church." notes

O'Brien, Terence, S.D.B. *Dominic Savio: Teenage Apostle and Saint.* New Rochelle, New York: Salesiana Publishers, 1969.

Papa, Rev. Dominic C.P., trans. *A Curved Bridge to Calvary.* Jamaica, New York: Vice Postulation Office, undated.

Piccorelli, S.J., Luciana Rivas. *27 Nuevos Santos Mexicanos.* Mexico City: Buena Prensa, 2000.

Pompilio, Stefano, C.P. *Beato Grimoaldo Santamaria. Castelliri*:
Tipografia Editrice Pasquarelli, 1995.

Roiz, Miguel Angel and Roiz, Carlos Villa. *De America al Cielo.*
Mexico, 1999.

Salaverri, José Maria. *Los Panes y Los Peces de Faustino.* Madrid:
Imprinta S.M., 1999.

Salaverri, José Maria. *Tal Vez Me Hable Dios.* Madrid: Ediciones
S.M., 1986.

Sanna, Don Giovanni. *Martirio E Vita della Beata Antonia
Mesina.* Oliena: Seristampa, 1995.

Scannel, Rev. *Little Nellie of Holy God.* Cork: Diocese of Cork,
undated.

Segarra, Ignatio. *Gente Que Hizo Mucho.* Barcelona: Editorial
Armonia, 1992.

Schweich, Mrs. R., trans. Basset, Madeleine. *Stairway to Heaven.*
Cannes: Dominican Sisters, undated.

Szczebak, Ks. Wladyslaw. *Sladami Blogoslawionej Karoliny
Kozkowny.* Tarnow: Diocese of Tarnow, 1998.

Uralde, Ca.Ch., Maria Louisa. *Teresita's Story.* Madrid: Causa de
Teresita, 1993.

Valabek, Redemptus M., O.Carm., *Profiles in Holiness, Vol. I and
II.* Roma: Edizioni Carmelitane, 1996 and 1999.

Verd-Conradi, Gabriel, S.J. *Mari Carmen González-Valero: A
Girl on Her Way to the Altars.* Madrid: Madres Carmelitas
Descalzas, undated.

Von Matt, Leonard and Bosco, Henri. *Don Bosco.* New York:
Universe Books, 1965.

Werbinski, Ks. I and Skoczylas, Ks. K. *Swieta Karolina.*
Wloclawek: Wydawnictwo Duszpasterstwa Rolnikow, 1997.

Wood, Robert D., S.M. *Maybe God Will Speak to Me.* (folio.
English translation of Salaverri's *Tal vez me hable Dios.*)
1993.

Zanzucchi, Michele. "Chiara Luce." *Living City*, May, 2000.
Vol. 39, No. 5, p. 15.

Zenit news release, "Anna Wang; Teen-age Martyr". *National
Catholic Register*, October 15-21, 2000. pp. 14-15.

_____ "Faithful ... Even to Giving One's Life: Lasallian Martyrology." *Bulletin of the Institute of the Brothers of the Christian Schools* No. 244. Rome: Generalate F.S.C., 1998.

_____ "Gérard Raymond: A Favored Soul." Quebec: *Friends of Gérard Raymond,* 1983.

_____ "Gérard Raymond: 1912-1932." Quebec: *Magnificat* Magazine. Vol XVII, No. 6.

THANK YOU

Rev. Campion Lally, O.F.M., Tokyo, Japan
Rev. Richard Flores, Ft. Worth, Texas
Rev. Dr. Ignacio Segarra, Barcelona, Spain
Discalced Carmelite Nuns, Aravaca, Spain
Rev. Anthony Anderson, SOLT, Corpus Christi, Texas
Mr. and Mrs. Tom George, Santa Rosa Beach, Florida
Sister Theresa Marie, O.P., Hawthorne, New York
Mrs. Amy Whitsell, Austin, Texas
Ms. Marigen Lohla, Focolare, San Antonio, Texas
Mariam Adams, Focolare, San Antonio, Texas
Rev. J. B. Itcaina, Missions Etrangeres de Paris, Rome, Italy
Joe and Jean Anne Hand, Nashville, Tennessee
Carol Pinard, Stamford, Connecticut
Salesian Missions, New Rochelle, New York
Brother Ralph Neumann, Noviciado Marianista, Queretaro, Mexico
Rev. Henricus Torres, S.M., Rome, Italy
José Maria Salavrerri, S.M., Valencia, Spain
Rev. Vinh Quang Nguyen, New Jersey
Rev. Jean-Guy Sauvageau, Seminaire de Quebec, Canada
Bill Moreau, C.S.B., Toronto, Canada
Rev. Vincent O'Malley
Rev. Paolo Molinari, S.J., Rome, Italy
Rev. Martin A. Hegyi, S.J., Fordham University, Bronx, New York
Rev. Chuong H. Nguyen, S.D.B.
Brother Rodolfo Meoli, F.S.C., Rome, Italy
Brother Alain Houry, F.S.C., Rome, Italy
Brother John Kavanagh, F.S.C. Archives, Rome, Italy
Mark Kohan, editor, *Polish American Journal*, New York
Stefania Moraczewska, Diocese of Wloclawek, Poland
Ann Bobak, Michigan
Rev. Boguslaw Wojcik, Diocese of Tarnow, Poland
Rev. Msgr. Zygmunt Zimowski, Rome, Italy

Rev. Joannes Zubiani, C.P., Rome, Italy
Julia Schmitt, Marcelini, Missouri
Sac. Pasquale Grecu, Nuoro, Italy
Anita Lewis, Passionist Historical Archives, Union City, New
    Jersey
Rev. Dominic Papa, C.P., Jamaica, New York
Fidelma Bulter, Waterford, Ireland
Sister Francis Xavier, Cork, Ireland
Jan Petkov, Opava, Czechoslovakia
Robert Nemec, Christnet, Czechoslovakia
Anna Tailanova, Pizen, Czechoslovakia
Rev. Redemptus Valabek, O.Carm, Rome
Rev. L. Belley, archivist, Missionaries of Africa, Montreal
Sister Maria Guadalupe Franco Sánchez, Las Palmas, Grand
    Canaries
Carol Pinard, Stamford, Connecticut
Mr. and Mrs. Joe Hand, Nashville, Tennessee
Rev. J. B. Itcaina, Missions Etrangeres de Paris, Rome, Italy
Brother John Kavanaugh, F.S.C. Archives, Rome, Italy
Brother Alain Houry, Rome, Italy
Mrs. Mary Alice Richard, Richard, Louisiana
Mrs. Fidelma Butler, Waterford, Ireland
Ms. Mary Francis Lester, Rockford, Illinois
Sister Francis Xavier, Sunday's Well, Ireland
Rev. José Maria Saliaverri, S.M., Colegia de N.S. del Pilar,
    Valencia, Spain
Brother Ralph Neumann, S.M., Noviciado Marianista,
    Queretaro, Mexico
Mia Jaoude, Tucson, Arizona
Anita Lewis, Passionist Archives, Union City, New Jersey
Rev. Francesco Guera, C.P., Convent of the Presentation,
    Orbetelo, Italy
Rev. Giovanni Zubiani, C.P., Postulator General for the
    Passionists, Rome, Italy
Rev. Martin Hegyi, Fordham University, Bronx, New York
Sister Teresa Marie, Rosary Hill Home, Hawthorne, New York
Ms. Anna Bobak, Harrison Township, Michigan
Stefania Moraczewska, Diocese of Wloclawek, Poland

Rev. Msgr. Zygmunt Zimowski, Rome, Italy
Rev. Boguslaw Wojcik, Diocese of Tarnow, Poland
Rev. Benjamin Fiore, S.J., Canisius College, Buffalo, New York
Chantal Pinchon, Friends of Anne de Guigné, Paris, France
Eugene Szynkowski, Roseville, Michigan
Brian Finnerty, Opus Dei, New Rochelle, New York
Yago de la Cierva, Opus Dei
The Gonsalez-Barros Family, Madrid, Spain
Rev. Anthony Anderson, SOLT, Corpus Christi, Texas
Ms. Rossana Gani, Denver, Colorado
Alejandro Bermudez, Lima, Peru
Mother of Sonia Diaz Parga
Grazia Casale, Vallo Torinese, Italy
Martin Roche
Marija Bonnici, Melbourne, Australia
Pierre and Gina Choueiry, Beirut, Lebanon
Bishop John Elya
Antoine Courban, Beirut, Lebanon
Mia Khoury-Aboujaoude,
Martha Liles
Paul Stamm, Milwaukee, Wisconsin
Pere Michel Abras, O.B.A., Sarba, Lebanon
Mrs. Nelly Medawar Baladi, Zouk Mikael, Lebanon
Rev. Pasquale Grecu, Nuoro, Italy
Rev. Simeone della S. Famiglia, O.C.D., Rome, Italy
Theresa Zheng, Liverpool, New York
Brother DePorres Stilp, M.M., Wilkes-Barre, Pennsylvania
Debra Wang, Corpus Christi, Texas
Rev. William Hart McNichols, Ranchos de Taos, New Mexico

INDEX OF HOLY PERSONS

GENERAL INDEX

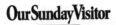

Our Sunday Visitor ...
Your Source for Discovering
the Riches of the Catholic Faith

Our Sunday Visitor has an extensive line of materials for young children, teens, and adults. Our books, Bibles, pamphlets, CD-ROMs, audios, and videos are available in bookstores worldwide.

To receive a FREE full-line catalog or for more information, call **Our Sunday Visitor** at **1-800-348-2440, ext. 3**. Or write **Our Sunday Visitor** / 200 Noll Plaza / Huntington, IN 46750.

Please send me ___ A catalog
Please send me materials on:
___ Apologetics and catechetics
___ Prayer books
___ The family
___ Reference works
___ Heritage and the saints
___ The parish

Name _____
Address _____ Apt._____
City _____ State _____ Zip_____
Telephone (   ) _____

                                            A43BBBBP

Please send a friend ___ A catalog
Please send a friend materials on:
___ Apologetics and catechetics
___ Prayer books
___ The family
___ Reference works
___ Heritage and the saints
___ The parish

Name _____
Address _____ Apt._____
City _____ State _____ Zip_____
Telephone (   ) _____

                                            A43BBBBP

OurSundayVisitor

200 Noll Plaza, Huntington, IN 46750
Toll free: **1-800-348-2440**
Website: www.osv.com